Guts:
The Lane Evans Story

Devin Hansen

STRONG ARM PRESS

WASHINGTON D.C.

D1453264

Cover Design: Mike Mathews, Serhan Urganci, Aleksandar Stanojevic and Devin
Hansen.
Cover Photo credit to Moline Dispatch
Publishing Co. Rights secured on 8-22-2016.
Cover Formatting by Paige Kelly
Book Design by Troy N. Miller

Copy Editor: Alex Abbott
Managing Editor: Troy N. Miller

Printed in the United States of America
First Edition

Published by Strong Arm Press
www.strongarmpress.com
Washington, DC

ISBN-13: 978-1-947492-40-0

To Lane -
The work goes on
The cause endures

Acknowledgements

There are many people who helped bring Lane's story to the public so forgive me for not acknowledging each and every one of you. First, thank you to Cher Erickson and Mike Malmstrom for allowing me to reconnect with Lane in his final years, and for their honesty, understanding, and commitment to Lane's well-being. Also, thank you to Lane's former staffers and friends for their heartfelt interviews, especially Jim Hightower, Jan Schakowsky, John Ayers, John Kuper, Phil Hare, Dennis King, and the great Fred Harris. Also thanks to Justin Farley and Jim Mertens for the audiobook; James Larrabee for early editing; and those who helped Lane move at the last-minute, Joe and Linda Bessera, Mike Chilemmi, Kellie Vogt, Andy Snead, Aaron Armes and Tony Armes. Thank you to Robert Creamer for introducing me to Ryan Grim, and thanks to Ryan, Alex Lawson, Troy Miller and the rest of the team at Strong Arm Press. This book is a result of ten years of research, interviews, and patience and is the highlight of my writing career. So thank you to my early writing teachers: JoAnn Nusbaum, and the late David R. Collins, Patty Newburg, B.J. Elsner, and David Foster Wallace. Most of all thank you to my wife for her love, encouragement and support, and to my children for giving me purpose.

Catherine I. Hansen, Devin Hansen, and Lane Evans – 1983

Contents

Chapter One

Nowhere Man

December 2008: The place was called the Lighthouse, a replica of which served as the entrance. A relatively new building flanked by subdivisions and storage units rather than coastline and ocean. Three-stories of single-unit apartments for seniors and the disabled. It was a step above the typical nursing home. There were no patients wandering aimlessly down the halls. No lobby full of invalids placated with a game of Hangman. All of these residents here were dressed for social hour. It was still a place of dignity.

I waited while the receptionist called Lane's room. In one hand was my briefcase and the other a poinsettia; a red one with foil around the pot. It was a thank-you gift for his main caretaker Cher Erickson. She was appointed as one of his guardians in 2007, along with Lane's former driver Mike Malmstrom. They were his first and last line of defense, there to stave off the con artists and the beggars, the ex-lovers and groupies driven by greed or morbid curiosity. I had to prove to Cher that I was legit, since she could put an end to the project right away.

I chewed three mints while waiting for her. More out of nerves than her tardiness. Soon she appeared in the lobby. A curvy blonde and in her late fifties; we met with a smile and handshake.

She asked about my background, my family, and how I first met Lane. It was like a job interview except there would be no salary. The congressman was broke, she told me. He barely had enough money to pay for his rent and medical care. He'd been too generous over the years and his pension was miniscule. This project would have to be a labor of love.

His near-poverty was the first surprise of many.

"Is there anything I *shouldn't* talk to him about?"

"His mother. He doesn't like talking about his mother. That brings him down."

"OK. But, I will have to ask him about the Parkinson's. You know, like where he could be..."

"If he didn't get sick?"

"Yeah."

"That's OK, you can talk about that."

A level of trust now between us, we took the elevator to the second floor. His apartment was at the end of a series of hallways. They were wide and clean and smelled like Christmas. Lane's door had a small stone set in the front etched with the Marine Corps logo.

"Just to let you know, he just woke up and hasn't showered yet," Cher said, turning the knob.

I took a step back.

"It's OK," she smiled, telling me not to worry. "It'll just have to be a short visit."

I followed her inside through a small kitchenette and into the living area. Everything was painted white. Several plaques and awards decorated the walls. There was a recliner, couch, and a floor-model television that dominated the room. Lane was dressed in a mismatched sweat-suit, hunched on the couch slowly swaying like a pianist.

Cher turned off the TV and I sat on the edge of the recliner.

"Hi, Lane," I said, nearly shouting. "How's it going?"

"You remember Devin," Cher said. "He brought us this flower." She set the poinsettia on the kitchen counter, next to three others just like it.

"It's just a small thanks for letting me meet with you, sir."

Lane mumbled something in reply. His eyes were still groggy and the right side of his hair was pushed up.

I told him my plans for the book and how I wanted to meet with him once a week. Lane replied in a mumbled whisper, which Cher had to translate: "Sounds good so far."

His mouth was anchored by the disease, often resulting in slobbering and incoherent mumbling. All around the apartment there were signs pronouncing: "Speak LOUD!"

I became aware of my own volume: "Do I have to be talking this loud? Can you hear OK, sir?"

"Yes, he hears OK. It kind of aggravates him when people think they have to shout," Cher said.

I apologized. Then we talked about the weather, the sleet falling outside, and other nonsense until I caught onto his speech pattern. It was a dry whisper with almost no annunciation. His lips were heavy, almost still. But soon with a little practice I could understand nearly every word.

"You had the cinema. I always enjoyed that place," he said, referring to a cinema-pub I had owned. It was across the street from one of his campaign offices and he would often come in to chat or watch a movie. It was the last place I'd seen him, many years ago.

"I can't stay long, so maybe you can give me some pictures to scan. Like when you were a kid and what not. Whatever you want to add to the book."

He agreed and Cher took me to his bedroom to show me some of his favorites. There were pictures of him with Julia Louis-Dreyfus, Bill Clinton, Michael J. Fox, and one of his heroes: Paul McCartney. It was then I started noticing all the Beatles posters and books. They were outnumbered only by the Marine decor. Awards, medals, the folded U.S. flag of his dead father. A lifetime in one tiny room. The only thing missing were photos of his family. Of children. The one legacy he wouldn't leave. It was a subject I forgot to ask Cher about—why had he never settled down?

We went back to the living room. I put the photos in my briefcase. Cher excused herself to the kitchen and sorted through his bevy of pills for the afternoon regimen. I had time for one more question - it had to be good:

"What makes a man?"

Lane was silent, staring at the floor. I waited. Unsure if it was because the question was stupid or if he was enduring one of his frequent hallucinations that Cher had told me about.

A minute passed and I asked again: "What makes a person great?"

His mouth opened but the only thing that came out was a string of saliva. I grabbed the towel from his lap and wiped it away. Then he turned his head up and looked at me, clearly wanting to answer. I looked at him directly in the eyes: "What does it mean to be human?"

"That-does-not-compute," he said in a robotic voice.

I laughed. He still had the wit. Though it wasn't quite as quick, it was the same dry, nerdy humor he had back when he was healthy.

"Sorry, I'm just trying to find out what quality you admire the most in people..."

This time something in his mind clicked: "Guts. I like guts. Be willing to stand up. To take a punch."

Guts. Hard-nosed, Semper-Fi, take-it-like-a-man, Guts!

Cher returned with his pills. After that it would be time for his physical therapy. So I held out my hand to say goodbye. He didn't reach for it. Instead he rocked back and forth in the sofa to gain momentum as Cher came over and grabbed him by the hands. One, two, three and he was up on his feet. His knees shook as he gained his balance.

He took a step toward me and we shook hands purposefully.

The consummate congressman.

"Bye, sir."

Down the elevator and through the lobby, I swallowed a few tears.

Guts.

The quality he most admired and most embodied. He had it in the Marines. He had it in Congress. And he had it during his final years moving from rest home to rest home, enduring the painful tremors of Parkinson's and time-bending hallucinations of Lewy body dementia. Madness and melancholy. His only connection to the world through that giant television that was endlessly blaring. And for a man with a genius-level IQ and a hyper-appetite for books, it was perhaps a fate worse than purgatory.

But there he waited. Taking it like a man.

Unfazed. Unbridled. Guts.

He would never admit this. Because if there's one thing that Lane Evans embodied even more, it was humility. And that combination of bravery and humbleness is what made him so successful in Congress. His modesty was endearing to his constituents and elicited a sense of trust among his Democratic and Republican colleagues.

He never pandered to voters and voted his conscience even if it wasn't politically expedient. If staffers would try to change his position on an issue merely for political gain, Lane would say: "People believe a believer." It was one of his favorite mantras.

"People can sniff out bullshit," he would say. "They can sniff out opportunistic politicians. People know that I believe in what I say and what I am doing."

Even something as simple as a haircut represented so much more. He had a boyish, unkempt bowl-cut that he kept for years after its expiration. When friends and strategists would tell him to cut it, he'd say: "I'm not gonna change my hair cause if I do then I'll start changing other things."

And after twenty-four years in Washington, Lane never changed. He stayed true to himself and his roots in Rock Island, Illinois, the rust-belt hometown that shaped him, educated him, and cemented his political views. Lane was always a Rock Islander — he just happened to spend a couple decades visiting D.C.

In a perfect world, Lane would be writing his own story, and much more eloquently I'm sure. But this is how fate worked out. I'm writing for a dead man who's still alive. A man who can barely speak or write. A nowhere man.

This is Lane Evans. As I know him.

Guts and all.

Chapter Two

Little Child

Rock Island is part of the Quad Cities, a metropolitan area of roughly 350,000 people spanning Iowa and Illinois on the Mississippi River. It is technically five cities, including Bettendorf and Davenport in Iowa; and Moline, East Moline and Rock Island in Illinois. It is surrounded by a number of small farming and industrial communities that stretch down along the river to Quincy, Illinois and once made up the 17th Congressional District of Illinois.

It is in the heart of flyover country, and though it has a population about the size of Des Moines and Omaha, it is ignored by the national media. For example, on news programs like *Good Morning America* and *The Today Show*, their weather maps display Des Moines and Omaha, then have a blank space where you should see the Quad Cities. We are so forgotten, that if a celebrity comes to town to play golf at the John Deere Classic or is spotted at a restaurant, it makes the local news.

It was once the farm-implement capital of the world and home to manufacturing plants for Case, Caterpillar, International Harvester, and John Deere & Company until the early 1980s, when nearly all these factories merged, closed, or slashed their workforce. Thirty years later, and the area is still recovering; only John Deere remains.

The Quad Cities is made up of these blue-collar, salt-of-the-Earth folks. They'll bore you to death with talk of NASCAR, but then rush to help you change a tire in the middle of the night. Today, the Quad Cities has become a collection of ethnicities and there has been a cultural revolution of sorts. A thriving arts community continues to grow, and it has a robust selection of live theater, comedy, and music. The demographics indicate it will continue to become more educated and diverse, especially with a recent influx of immigrants and refugees. However, even with a growing minority population, there is still a divide. This is especially true in Rock Island, where the majority of its middle-class and white citizens live "above the hill," while the low-income and minorities are segregated "below the hill."

While the Quad Cities may be diverse, its backyard barbeques are still very monochromatic.

This is where Lane Evans was born on August 4, 1951: Rock Island. His father Lee was a Navy veteran and firefighter who worked several secondary jobs from carpentry to pest control. His mother Jocelyn (Joyce) was a homemaker, nurse, and Democratic precinct committeewoman. They were married in 1948 and would raise four sons: Steve, Lane, and years later, Doyle and Dave.

Lane's father was athletic and hardworking and was often humming or whistling around the house. He was also friendly, kind, and had a reputation for honesty and trustworthiness. He instilled these same qualities into Lane and his brothers. Joyce, who had gone back to school in her forties to become a nurse practitioner, worked at a community health clinic and volunteered at local hospice centers.

Growing up, they watched the news religiously, and the dinner table was filled with political conversations. "Politics were our sports," Doyle recalled. "My bike even had a Humphrey sticker on it." Lee was a big supporter of unions and firefighters and quietly worked in the background, while Joyce was active and outspoken, even recruiting the boys to help her campaign for local Democrats. From their earliest days, the kids would hand out literature door to door, lick envelopes or sit with her at information tables outside of grocery stores.

Joyce once said: "I just like politics and I like government and I think I helped instill that in Lane. I think the gentle, caring part of him came from his dad. I'm more outgoing than all of my family put together."

Lane looked up to his older brother, Steve. When John F. Kennedy stumped in the Quad Cities in October of 1959, Joyce took the two boys to watch his motorcade as it slowly traveled across the Centennial Bridge from Davenport to Rock Island. JFK reached out from the car window and shook Steve's hand as the eight-year-old Lane watched awestruck. The fleeting moment had a huge impact on the two boys, inspiring them both to serve their country.

Joyce tried to instill a love of civics in her sons and encouraged all of them to enter politics, but ultimately Lane was the only one who ever tried to get his name on a ballot. The other boys pursued their own dreams. Lane had the same passion for politics as Joyce did, and she fanned that flame.

His mother was revered in the Quad Cities, winning several awards for her civic efforts and volunteer work. She helped thousands of people and was often referred to as angelic, but behind closed doors she was often cruel to Lane, mentally and emotionally. Some say it was because she had her own unresolved issues from a traumatic childhood and tried to mask it with strength and control, pushing Lane harder than the other boys. But Lane never felt any regret or anger towards her. To the day he died, the mere mention of his mother would bring tears to his eyes. He called her a "pit bull" and said that she pushed him out of love.

Lane's childhood was predominantly happy and comfortable, though. He wanted for nothing and attended private Catholic school. He spent his days hanging out with two of his best friends and class-mates, Steve Brinn and Bill Logan. They played Risk, explored the ravines, and rode their bikes nonstop around Rock Island. Once, Lane's father even indulged Brinn, Logan and Lane with a trip to Chicago's Comiskey Park to see The Beatles in 1965. The boys shared a pair of binoculars from their outfield seats, watching a daytime show that was barely audible, yet unforgettable. "That was the most exciting thing I could imagine," Lane recalled. "The music gave me a way of expressing myself and it was very much political."

After graduating from middle school Lane surprised everyone by entering the seminary. His mother was pushing him toward politics, yet at the same time she felt service to the Church could be equally as important. Joyce would often host parties at the home for other ded-icated "church ladies" and the parish priest. One of the more liberal priests, Father Real, would attend those parties. The Catholic church had recently adopted sweeping changes known collectively as, "Vat-ican II," including increasing outreach and converting the mass into local languages (as opposed to Latin). Father Real supported Vatican II and had turned the church rectory into a Catholic Worker House. This commitment to the poor resonated with Lane, and that may have been the inspiration to join the seminary.

But after just two short weeks, Lane abruptly quit and returned home. He never said why he left the seminary and never implied that anything inappropriate happened. He just said it wasn't what he expected and it was just a "small part of his life."

Lane then enrolled at Alleman Catholic High School in Rock Island, about half a mile from his home. Alleman is a school that breeds success: it has strong community roots, and its list of alma mater features numerous lawyers, doctors, entrepreneurs, and pol-iticians. It is a tight-knit community where students are held ac-countable for their actions and parents are regularly involved. It is also a place where exposure to economic and racial diversity is quite slim. So, while it surpasses most schools in terms of curriculum and education, it lacks in readying students for the challenges of a diverse American culture.

Lane attended Alleman during its most popular years in the late 1960s when the school had nearly 1400 students. That number has hovered around four hundred in recent years, but little else has changed. The basketball court is still made of the same polished wooden boards. There is still a giant green "A" in the marble of the entryway, the same dented metal trash cans are in the restrooms and, of course, Father Mirabelli still wanders the halls.

Mirabelli is synonymous with Alleman High School, where he has worked since 1966 as an educator, celebrant, and Director of Development. He attends every sporting event, remembers every student, and looks like a grey-haired leprechaun.

"I had Lane in my history class for political thinkers. He was an excellent student and always well prepared," Father Mirabelli said. "He really studied people. He had insight into the lives of people. He was a very diligent young man. There was something about him that attracted you to him. He had a quality of understanding and kindness."

"He never forgot he came from Alleman," Mirabelli said. "He always sent us something special from his office for auctions. Whenever we needed American flags for the pole outside, he'd send one about three days later. He told me they flew over Washington, and I told him, 'I know.'"

Though well-liked by his classmates, Lane was also very shy. In group pictures he is always in the back, peeking over shoulders and keeping his head low. Lane would still join in activities like decorating the homecoming float, cheering on the sports teams, or hanging out at the Italian Village and watching girls. Still, he preferred spending time with his close friends Brinn and Logan, playing board games and discussing politics, and his weeknights were often spent alone reading history books. Lane also worked after school, helping his dad with one of his many side jobs. One year, Lane helped his father spraying insecticides; a job that some say would come back to affect the health of both of them many years later.

Overall, Lane had a reputation as a thinker. Especially a political thinker. During his senior year he helped his friend and popular athlete Steve VanSpeybroeck get elected class president. Lane would never run for Student Council, preferring to stay in the background like a savvy political operative.

"Lane would have been voted the least likely kid to go to Congress. He was very unassuming," VanSpeybroeck remembered. "He was just not the kind of guy you thought would be in the political life. He was just one of the guys."

In 1969, Lane graduated in the largest class that Alleman has ever known. It was also one of the most turbulent, formative years in the United States. The beginning of the culture wars. And Lane would take the first steps to his political career by joining the United States Marine Corps.

Chapter Three

Twist & Shout

December 2008: Three questions per week. That was the plan. I'd write them on a sheet of paper and put it under a magnet on the fridge so Lane could prepare his answers whenever he felt lucid. Then I'd return the following Tuesday to discuss them. Usually before lunch and after physical therapy, one of the few times in the day he was alert (according to Cher Erickson, one of his official guardians and main caretakers).

They would be philosophical questions. About his emotions and his insights of the past. I could get all the facts and figures from his friends and staffers, but his feelings had to come firsthand.

I knocked. A twenty-something stranger answered the door. He had crooked teeth and a hamburger belly. Confused, I asked: "Where's Cher?"

"She'll be back." He stared at me dumbly.

"I'm here to interview Lane...You know. About the book?"

He shrugged ignorantly and let me in. There was a physical therapist (PT) stretching Lane in the living room, who grunted and sighed with each twist and turn. A painful display of human origami. It was meant to keep him limber and prolong his mobility by relieving the tightness and trembling.

"I can quit, if you need to talk to him," he said as he pushed Lane's left foot toward the ceiling.

I told him that I could wait; continue with the gentle torture.

I sat at the kitchen counter and talked with the kid. He had graduated high school a few years ago and was now one of Lane's part-time caretakers. His job was to feed Lane, take him to the bathroom and make sure he didn't accidentally hurt himself. He was basically a glorified babysitter. Lane drools, he sleeps most of the day, suffers from dyskinesia (the trembling) and wears adult diapers. But unlike watching a child, there is no potential for growth or improvement

19

and the job will only get more difficult.

Over time, Lane's muscles would continue to tighten. Perhaps his teeth would fall out due to the Parkinson's drugs. His mind would continue to cloud. And soon, his throat muscles might fail and he wouldn't be able to swallow. He'd then be on a feeding tube. And after that, a breathing tube. If and when he reached that point, he'd need more qualified care, but for now his needs were tended.

Cher spends one eight-hour shift with Lane and is continually looking for part-timers to cover the other two shifts. The main qualifications are that they don't steal Lane's prescriptions, and that they show up to work. Since the pay is just $8.50 an hour, that limits the number of honest applicants, so she takes what she can get.

At first, Lane was not happy about his 24/7 care. He felt he could still care for himself. He wanted that independence. He used to tell Cher: "I don't need this, I don't need these people around." He began to push away the helpers and even go so far as locking them out of his apartment if he didn't like them.

Cher had to prove to him that he needed the round-the-clock attention. "I would tell him, 'Go get your own lunch. Go get your own pills. Go to the bathroom by yourself.' Then I'd go sit in the hall for thirty minutes at a time, just to let him see he couldn't do it himself." She'd watch and wait, and when Lane finally came to his own realization, she would step in: "I had to play hardball with him at first to show him he needed help."

Lane had finally realized that needing help didn't mean surrender.

Thirty minutes passed and the PT finished. The Tin Man had been oiled. Lane was sweaty and limber. They took a walk through the halls, Lane's arms pumping like a speed-walker but moving at an elderly pace. They went to one end of the building and back again. It drained him. Lane fell into his couch and panted. The PT gave him a high-five and said he'd see him again in a couple days.

After he caught his breath, I grabbed my laptop and sat beside the congressman. He said something inaudible between breaths. I leaned in to listen.

"Lane wants to know what's for lunch," I called to the kitchen.

The kid showed him a cellophane-wrapped plate of baked chicken, mashed potatoes and green beans that the Lighthouse had delivered.

"What's the other option?" Lane asked.

The kid went to the fridge, then shrugged at us over the door.

Lane sighed. The kid came over to feed him, but I said I could do it. I grabbed a spoon and ripped off the plastic. He ate like a growing toddler. Spoon after spoon, until his cheeks couldn't hold any more, then he swallowed and opened his mouth again. His plate was clean in less than five minutes.

I wiped his mouth, and then gave him a can of Diet Pepsi with a bendable straw. Drinking was one of the few things he could still do on his own.

"Ready for the interview?" I smiled.

He nodded and carefully set down the can. I grabbed the sheet of questions I had left for him the past week on the fridge, hoping he and Cher had reviewed them.

"Question number one. Are you still a Catholic?"

"Well, I do and I don't hold my faith close. I don't have time to do the kind of obvious things that Catholics do, I guess."

His mind quickly wandered and his words followed: "I was in the Marine Corps part of the time you know so it never really loosened my faith. They have a real important role to play and I think they do quite well. I'm not. They'll be able to make their impact on younger Catholics. I think I've probably said more now than in years. That was part of the program. Being ostracized, you know."

I captured every word, no matter how disjointed.

"Question two. Who knew you best?"

"My mother did. Probably now Erin. She's been into my issues and story. Who knows my story? You too this point. And who was always there like my mother, it's now Erin that fills those shoes."

Erin Saberi. His longtime girlfriend, now living in California. I emailed her a few times, and she said she'd visit in a few short weeks. She had described their relationship as the "fundamental relationship in both our lives."

"OK Lane, last question. Why do you love Rock Island?"

"Rock Island has everything that a city should be. It's different in terms that it has everything anyone who would ever want in a city. People more so in the past, but they are still there, the people are good."

As I typed, Lane slowly eased back into the couch, his eyes closing.

I stacked a few pillows nearby and gently pushed him into the pile. The kid turned on the television and sat nearby. He asked Lane what he wanted to watch, but the congressman was already asleep.

A few days later, I popped in unannounced. A blond caretaker I didn't know answered. I introduced myself and slid past her. She sat down at the kitchen counter littered with puzzle pieces and old Christmas candy. Lane was sitting on the couch watching *A Few Good Men* and dressed in a sweatshirt with the Marines emblem on the front. I wanted to crack a joke, but he was actually pretty engrossed in the movie.

"Hey, Lane!" I sat next to him. My weight dipped the cushions and sent him slowly toward me. I caught his shoulder and braced a pillow under his elbow.

"Is this your day to come here?" he mumbled, not looking away from the movie.

"No, I was just in the neighborhood and thought I'd stop by," I said somewhat embarrassed. Lane was not one for spontaneity.

"This is the good part," he called (surprisingly loudly) to the caretaker. She nodded without looking. Tom Cruise was on the TV grilling Jack Nicholson.

"I'm sorry for just dropping by. I know you like your schedules."

"It's OK. It's tenacious. We have a working relationship now."

I eased into the couch and decided to leave my computer in my backpack. We watched the movie for awhile. Both of us making jokes and comments. His were far funnier than mine.

Suddenly it hit him... a barrage of muscle cramps.

I jumped off the couch and watched. His fists clenched and his body went fetal. Eyes pinched. His mouth gaped but silent. His chin quivered, like a child sucking in the breath before a wail. Then, he pressed his lips together and let out a sound that had to be heard to be understood. A guttural hum. A stifled scream buried deep in his diaphragm and then slowly released between two clenched jaws.

It was a horrific moan that no actor could ever replicate.

Think about the pain of a single cramp, and then multiply that by the six hundred and fifty muscles in your body. You don't know when it's going to happen, or when it's going to end. And it's so commonplace that the people around you have become desensitized to your pain. It truly is torture.

When it was over, I sat beside him. He panted through his nose and slowly opened his eyes. He blinked a few times and finished with a long sigh.

I expected some quip like, "Did I miss anything?" But he just looked back at the TV.

The movie ended. The girl never did look up from that puzzle. It happened so often, I assumed, she'd become unfazed.

"I think I'm going to rest now," he said.

I left without saying a word, feeling like I was going to vomit.

Chapter Four

Young Blood

They say the first day of Marine boot camp is the most degrading day of your life. This may be true. But for Lane Evans, it was a baptism. An entry into an elite brotherhood whose comradery and discipline stayed with him until death.

It was sixteen days after high school graduation when Lane enlisted in the Corps, following in the tradition of service set forth by his Navy-veteran father and Marine brother Steve. And like his short stint in the seminary, Lane saw the military as his path into public service. He'd be serving God and country at the same time.

It was 1969. Lane attended the Marine Corps Recruit Depot at Camp Pendleton in San Diego, rather than the older, more historic MCRD on Parris Island, South Carolina. Recruits sometimes joke that Camp Pendleton produces beach-loving Hollywood Marines, while Parris Island is for the men who don't mind fleas, snakes and swamps. It's a friendly rivalry, of course, and as Lane said, "A Marine is a Marine no matter where he got his training."

After boot camp, Lane was stationed in Okinawa, Japan. He would have gone straight to Vietnam, but his brother Steve was already there. The Sullivan Act, enacted after World War II, disallowed any siblings from simultaneously serving in combat. Lane felt a sense of guilt about this for his entire life. He said he would have traded places with Steve in a minute. But he'd never taste war, smell torture, or wipe a man's brains off his flak jacket. This may explain Lane's deep dedication to veterans' issues while in Congress; a mixture of guilt and regret for something he could not control. And a sympathy for his brethren who had to experience it.

In 1971 Lane was honorably discharged. He was just twenty years old and had matured immensely over those two short years. He had been indoctrinated with the Marine culture of service and loyalty, and was exposed to cultures far different than those of his sheltered childhood. The Marines had taught him many lessons he would have never learned elsewhere. The once quiet, introverted boy now had a small taste of the world. And it gave him confidence.

"The Marines made me more aware," he said. "I didn't know many black or other ethnic groups growing up, so it really made me open my eyes. It was one of my best educations." And though he loved the Marines, he added: "I also learned I didn't want to be a Marine the rest of my life."

Lane then went to Black Hawk College, a state-run community college in Moline, Illinois. It was the logical first step for a working-class kid on the GI Bill to begin his secondary education. He took the general courses of Math, English and Humanities, and quickly received his Associate's Degree. He then attended Augustana College in 1972, a prestigious Lutheran college in Rock Island just down the hill from his childhood home, where he again lived with his parents.

Lane studied law and politics, while earning his political education outside the classroom by volunteering for Democratic candidates on the local and national level. He went door to door for one of the first black candidates for Rock Island city council, James Davis. (He lost, but years later would be elected Mayor.) Then in 1972 he dove headfirst into the George McGovern presidential campaign. He met Terry Knoch and Kevin Sullivan, two younger Alleman graduates who became his best friends. They worked at McGovern's campaign headquarters in a small room at the Fort Armstrong Apartments in Rock Island.

Lane and Sullivan remembered it as being one of the most haphazard campaigns they'd ever seen. Most of their time was sitting around trying to figure out what to do.

"The campaign was rudderless, to say the least," Sullivan said. "We couldn't even get stamps for mailers! Everyone looked like hippies. Lane and I were the most conservative-looking of the bunch. We actually had buttons and collars on our shirts. No one there knew what to do. But then one day we were all sitting around and we just decided to call and ask McGovern to make an appearance. And they said, OK!"

The campaign was energized. They had a purpose. "Somehow, someway, that chaotic organization got George McGovern to come to the Quad Cities on the Sunday before the election," Sullivan said. "It validated the campaign office. The advance-men arrived and we got our things organized. Lane and I finally had something real to do. We helped with parking, we set up the stage, and the Democratic leadership even came out. Lane and I got to shake hands with McGovern, but then the big boys took over."

This was Lane's first exposure to a major political organization. But as Sullivan said, "If Lane learned anything from the '72 campaign it was what *not* to do."

Of course, McGovern eventually lost in a landslide and Lane returned to focusing on his studies. Sullivan and Knoch remained close friends, spending hours with Lane in his parents' basement arguing politics, reading, and listening to music. Lane had a library and would read voraciously – economics, politics, and philosophy. He devoured books as he listened to album after album by The Beatles. Sometimes he'd take breaks to do push-ups, sit-ups, or take a short jog. Mental and physical fitness were his obsession. Cleanliness, however, was not.

"Lane was a slob. Pretty soon he moved out of his folks' and got a tiny little apartment and tried cramming all his books in there. It was chaos," said Sullivan.

"Lane was so single-minded. When he focused on something he was a laser," Knoch remembered. "He just wanted to get great grades. He could care less what shirt he was wearing, or even if it was clean."

Amid the apartment rubbish were boxes of file folders that contained news clippings, notes and other information on issues that concerned Lane. He also had files on many people's lives such as local politicians, national figures, and strangely, one for each of his friends. Not for blackmail nor revenge; they contained old Christmas cards and other mementos. "The man had boxes filled with research on political issues and the people who meant the most to him," Sullivan recalled. "At that moment, I knew he was meant for greatness."

Unlike many other college students, Lane didn't experiment heavily with drugs and alcohol. People say he stayed away from all of those distractions due to his upbringing and convictions. Most of his friends were activists or outcasts. Girls weren't far from their mind, just far from their attainment. So, music and politics were their time-killers. His idea of a fun weekend was buying a new record or visiting the library. One of the few places he did let loose was at Lee's in Rock Island, the local hotspot for students and just about everyone else in town.

"We hung out there all the time," Knoch said. "Beer was fifteen cents a glass. He'd have a couple but you'd never see him drunk. He was pretty good-sized man, so it never affected him. We would stay out till the place closed and then go to some place for breakfast or my place to debate."

Debates were his passion. Today he would have been venting on blogs and social media, but back then it was just him and his friends debating face to face. They'd crank a Beatles' record and then three guys would scream at each other about current events or, as Lane called them, "The great issues that face this nation."

"Lane would argue a point he didn't believe in, just to argue," Sullivan said. "We would scream incessantly and have a blast. Lane and Knoch would gang up against me and vice versa. It was a knock-down, drag-out fight," Sullivan laughed. "This was the foundation of his debating skills."

Lane usually won these debates by deflating his opponents with one statement, in true Lane Evans fashion: "I don't agree with you, but I respect your right to hold such an erroneous position."

These years were formative for Lane, and in 1974 he graduated *magna cum laude* from Augustana. The Marine was ready to head East and continue his studies, as well as his battles: "Lane was in a different place," as Knoch recalled. "He didn't get bothered with being an artist or musician. He was focused on one thing -- preparing himself intellectually to participate in the culture war."

From 1974 to 1977, Lane attended Georgetown University in his adoptive city of Washington D.C., where he met his good friend and future Chief of Staff, Dennis King. Lane was attending the university on his GI Bill and a few small student loans. He lived in a small boarding house the first year, with several political pages, and then a small efficiency apartment the next. His neighborhood was out of a movie, with decrepit buildings, random gunshots, and liquor stores open late into the night. But Lane fit in with his unkempt hair and ever-present army jacket. Scurrying from class to apartment and back again, he spent days reading, studying and eating whenever he remembered. Stacks of nonfiction were piled on the floor next to his mattress, and his cupboard held only canned beans and vegetables. "Eating is just a biological function," he used to say. Furniture and a telephone were unnecessary luxuries. His one prized possession was a small record player.

Sometimes Dennis would treat him to a movie, or he'd browse the record store and spend his meager food budget. Classes and study groups made up the bulk of his social interaction. Lane was viewed as peculiar, but still one of the nicest guys on campus. While many of the other students were obsessed with their own success and, as Dennis put it, "making corporate dough," Lane was focused on government service and politics, promising to fight for the little guys rather than cash in on his Georgetown golden ticket.

In 1975 Lane put this belief into practice, as he took a semester to work on the presidential campaign for Fred Harris. It was one of the defining campaigns he would ever be involved with, and helped shape his outlook on governance and grassroots activism.

Fred Harris was easily the most progressive candidate in the 1976 presidential race, stumping across the nation in a rented RV with his campaign manager Jim Hightower, the now-famous populist from Texas. He also ran in 1972 as a last-minute candidate, mostly to voice his concerns about Vietnam; but 1976 was a true campaign.

Harris was born in Oklahoma to a sharecropping family. He was elected to the state Senate in his early thirties, and then served in the U.S. Senate from 1964-1973. He was campaigning for Universal Health Care, a progressive tax system, and an end to corporate subsidies which he said "was a redistribution of wealth in the wrong direction."

Lane started as a grunt. A foot soldier. And since the campaign barely had enough cash to fuel the RV, Lane and his fellow volunteers were literally living hand-to-mouth, sleeping in campaign offices or in the backs of station wagons as they traveled from town to town. Lane was going door-to-door engaging people on a personal level and setting up information booths outside of grocery stores.

This was all comfortable to Lane. So much so, that at one point he was offered the coveted job of an advance-man, the person who visits campaign stops three days ahead of time, wears a suit, and organizes the locals. Lane declined by saying: "We win this thing on the ground!"

Lane so fervently believed in the campaign that it even cost him one of his closest friends. During a stop in Northern Illinois, Lane called Terry Knoch, and asked him to round up five hundred dollars and join the caravan. As Knoch recalled: "I had a great job at the time, and Lane wanted me to quit. I didn't do that and he got pissed off and said he didn't want to be friends! I had an apartment with a couch and a lamp and Lane wasn't interested in couches and lamps. He thought I sold out to the Republican establishment because I had a couch and lamp. He berated me about it. He was an absolute radical liberal, which I guess inspired him to do what he did in life. He helped disenfranchised people and was driven by the highest motives. Almost like someone who studied to be a priest. He had that kind of commitment."

One of Lane's fellow traveling volunteers was John Ayers, a college dropout and the product of a wealthy Chicago family. The two quickly became friends, bonding over their contempt for the ruling class despite their opposite upbringing. Lane called him one of the "cake-eaters" but respected Ayers' political skills and fundraising abilities.

Lane learned from Ayers and Harris how to convey complex issues in a way that the everyday voter could understand, without coming across as snobbish or overly intellectual. Harris had a knack for framing issues in a class context, which Lane studied and examined with Ayers as they drove the highways. At campaign rallies, attendees might even see conservatives nodding their heads at what Harris was saying. Lane took mental notes on everything he did and how the crowd reacted.

Harris ended up in fourth place in Iowa, and his populist message didn't go over well in New Hampshire. He ended up getting just nine delegates at the national convention.

"Lane had this ability to reach out to all sorts of people," Jim Hightower recalled. "He got it at a gut level, at an instinctive-level. He used that in the Harris campaign and then naturally kept that momentum going to build his own possibilities...That's the nature of these campaigns. They inspire people. Lane got inspired."

Other politicians were influenced by Harris too, sometimes without even knowing it. Jimmy Carter borrowed Harris' line, "Up with those who are down," which was also co-opted by John Edwards decades later. Even President Barack Obama often used the phrase "Now is the Time," which was the title of a 1971 book by Harris.

Fred Harris is now a political science professor at the University of New Mexico, of which Hightower quipped: "Lane and I used to say that we made Fred what he is today, a professor in Albuquerque."

Harris said Lane was one of the best things that happened in his campaign for president and probably the best by-product of that campaign. "When he was in Congress, it was almost like I was there too," Harris said.

After the campaign, Lane, Ayers and other young Harris volunteers were at a bar in Philadelphia discussing their futures. Ayers talked of returning to Chicago, while other volunteers talked about possible jobs they had lined up. Lane said that after he finished school, he was going to go back home and run for Congress. Ayers recalled: "We were all like, 'Yeah, whatever', that's a Republican county.' Then Lane said, 'I'm going to build a political base and I'll be in Congress by the early 1980s.'"

The rest of the kids laughed. Ayers could tell he was dead serious.

Lane graduated from Georgetown University Law Center in 1977 with his Juris Doctor degree, and returned to the Quad Cities to begin his career. He had a brief stint at Community Legal Clinic and the Western Illinois Legal Assistance Foundation. Then he joined Prairie State Legal Services in the new Martin Luther King Jr. Community Center in Rock Island, where they offered pro-bono legal services to minorities and the poor, and were counsel for local chapters of the NAACP and ACLU.

He was paid a mere eight thousand dollars a year and primarily worked on behalf of people facing foreclosure or eviction, workers with labor disagreements, and women who were victims of domestic abuse. The cases that involved battered women and children were his top priority, and for decades he held onto many of those early "thank you" letters and drawings. He remembered it as one of the most rewarding times in his life.

In 1980, Lane volunteered for Sen. Edward "Ted" Kennedy's presidential campaign while still working a few cases on the side. He became friends with a stout, mustached man named Phil Hare. The two had met briefly during the Harris campaign and now they would forge a strong relationship. And their roles were defined from the start: Lane was the leader and Phil was the sidekick.

"I really got to know him and watch him. He was such a smart guy," Phil recalled. "I got to see how much he knew about politics and the great things he did as a legal-aid attorney. I remember the old folks would come to him and ask to do their wills and he wouldn't take money from them. He handled a lot of cases for battered women and our local was about ninety-five percent women. Domestic violence was one thing that he was not going to tolerate."

The two men worked together in the trenches, applying lessons from the Harris campaign and still trying to "win it on the ground." But Jimmy Carter ended up demolishing Kennedy in the Illinois primary and the small group of volunteers was left without a candidate. That is until someone in the crowd scrawled out a makeshift political sign that read "Lane Evans for Congress."

Lane and Phil had earlier discussed the possibility several times while driving around the state. Though it had been on his mind since Georgetown, when pressed with the question, Lane played coy and turned the attention away from himself.

Then, a few weeks after the primary, Phil and his wife Becky decided to host a get-together at their home with the secret intention of convincing Lane to run for Congress.

"We had talked on the road a lot about it, so then one night I had him over to my house. It was my sisters and their husbands, and about eight other people. Becky made lasagna and we all played Crazy 8's. Then we all talked to him about running," Phil recalled.

It was almost like an intervention, but Lane didn't need much encouragement. He was going to make good on that promise he made to his classmates at Georgetown and already started one of his "folders" of notes and news clippings on the current congressman.

"We passed around my baseball hat and collected eighty-four dollars to start the campaign," Phil said. The very first Lane Evans for Congress meeting had occurred and the young liberal lawyer was going to take on the eight-term Republican incumbent, Tom Railsback, in a district that had been in Republican hands for all but two terms since the turn of the century.

Everyone figured Lane was a sacrificial lamb.

Chapter Five

A Day in the Life

January 2009: Lane Evans takes eleven different prescriptions for a daily total of about forty pills. Some are meant to numb, others are meant to heal, but mostly they just reduce the pain and trembling. This bevy of drugs makes Lane sleep more than the average housecat...

On a typical morning, he starts with a small breakfast and his first round of pills. This followed by a short sponge-bath, or the caretaker will simply freshen his armpits with a damp washcloth. He then watches a little television and has his first nap of the day. By late-morning he awakens for a visit from the physical therapist for an hour of intense stretching, light resistance training and a short walk. He then has lunch, another round of pills, and settles in for his afternoon nap. The rest of the day he goes in and out of consciousness, watching television or listening to music. Then he has dinner, another set of pills and either falls asleep on the couch or makes it to his bed.

He is constantly tired and confused, which is in stark contrast to other "Parkies," many of which still travel or go to movies and experience life. Many even still work, such as celebrities like Michael J. Fox — who still gets acting roles. The major difference between Lane and them, is that Lane also suffers from Lewy body dementia, so his symptoms are compounded by the hallucinations.

Some days he is alert, vocal, and aware. Other days he is lethargic, disoriented and barely able to move. As an outsider, I see no rhyme or reason to the causation. Sometimes he'll play pranks on his caretakers, or hide things and make jokes. Other times he can barely hold up his head.

Both Cher and Malmstrom said he has "good days and bad days." If there were a special event on the calendar, such as a Labor Day picnic, a funeral or a birthday party he would typically be having

31

one of his "good days." Did he battle his way through the pain and confusion? Or did they just skip some medications?

Cher and Malmstrom attributed it to his attitude: "He still rises to the occasion when he needs to. Especially when people are going to be talking about politics." Earlier in his career, Lane hinted at the fact that the symptoms were sporadic as well: "It comes and goes as it wants. You just deal with it. It is a very humbling illness to go through."

The couch is where he spends most of his time, watching CNN, *Seinfeld*, or Monty Python videos. Getting him up to walk or engage in physical therapy takes an outside trigger. A stimulus to get his mind and body moving. You had to grab him by the arms and pull him off the couch, then tap his feet to get them going. Once he does start to move, it takes him great effort to stop without falling. He usually ends his walks by literally falling into the couch cushions.

He has lost the ability to do what he wants, when he wants; something as simple as scrambling an egg, making popcorn, or even putting a fork to his lips. His days, his hours, his minutes were all at the mercy of dyskinesia, drugs and dementia.

Doctors try to control the shaking and the pain as much as possible. They prescribe a variety of drugs to find the perfect combination via trial-and-error. A drug that takes away one symptom might cause a different side effect that requires yet another drug. If they prescribe him drugs to control the dyskinesia, it may make him so tired he sleeps for hours. If they prescribe drugs to keep him alert, he could shake and shiver all day. It requires continuous oversight, and frankly, it's hard to tell if any of them know what the hell they're doing. Some friends said that it was more like a game of whack-a-mole than a definitive form of treatment.

Shortly after our initial interviews I started to drop in unannounced, mostly because I enjoyed talking to him, but also to catch the unscripted moments. To see the grit and grime. It didn't take long before I'd find him unchanged and unbathed, reeking of filth, with sores on his body, but only when the young caretakers were watching him. Some of them would let Lane sit in his own filth for hours, then clean him up right before Cher arrived. Sometimes Lane would complain. But for the most part he simply endured. Drugged, hallucinating, or hypnotized by the television.

I struggled with this, unsure of my role. So, I waited and watched, like some nature photographer watching a fawn drown in the river. It was my job to document, not to interject. At least, that's how I justified my inaction.

One afternoon I stopped by unannounced with the excuse of returning some photos that I had scanned for the book. One of the young girls answered the door. The one who liked puzzles.

I held up the stack of photos. "I wanted to return these before they got ruined."

"OK," she said, letting me in. I set the photos on the counter next to her puzzle.

Lane wasn't on the couch. He was in his bedroom. The door was nearly closed. I went over and peeked inside. He was on the edge of his bed. Shirtless, in sweatpants, with his hair disheveled.

He didn't notice me peeking in the doorway and kept staring straight ahead.

All his drawers were open. And empty. All of his clothes were stacked in piles across the floor, the bookshelves and stereo speakers.

"He's been like that all day," the girl said from the kitchenette. "He thinks people are stealing from him."

I gently opened the door: "Hi Lane."

He didn't move.

"I just stopped by to drop off some photos."

His head slowly turned toward me. There was no smile. No recollection nor recognition.

After staring at me for a moment, he gazed at the wall again. Blink. Blink. Breathe.

"OK, I gotta go now..."

Nothing.

"Bye, Lane," I said louder. Still nothing. I left the door open and then turned and left, walking quickly past the girl and through the lobby. I barely held in the tears until I made it to my truck.

I had never seen such a void. Such vast hopelessness in a man's eyes. Such confusion and disbelief. When he looked at me, his eyes said: "This is me. This is what I live with. And I don't know why."

Chapter Six

You Can't Do That

In 1966, Moline native Tom Railsback was elected to the United States Congress to represent the 19th district of Illinois, which was redrawn to become the 17th district after the 1980 census and stretched south from the Quad Cities to Macomb, and then east to Peoria and LaSalle-Peru. Railsback had defeated one-term Democrat Gale Schisler 52 percent to 48 percent after having served four years in the Illinois House, two years in the Army, and graduating from Northwestern University School of Law.

Railsback was generally well respected in the district due to his moderate Republican stance; he even received small campaign contributions from local labor unions and the United Automobile Workers. He voted against his party on issues like juvenile justice reform and funding new weapons programs, once saying that the nation was "becoming paranoid" with its increase in defense spending. Railsback spoke out against President Ronald Reagan's proposed cuts to social services programs in order to revive the B-1 bomber program, saying: "One plane costs more than the entire legal services program," which included Lane Evans' old employer, Prairie State Legal Services.

In 1974 Railsback gained national notoriety as a member of the House Judiciary Committee when he voted in favor of one of the articles of impeachment against President Richard Nixon. *Time* magazine named him one of the top two hundred future leaders of America, but this move angered many hardcore partisan Republicans in the district and many said it would haunt him in future elections.

Still, by all measures, Railsback was considered unbeatable. He had easily won seven reelection campaigns, with the biggest margin being 73 percent to 27 percent against Thomas Hand in 1980. Retirement seemed to be the only way he'd ever leave office, and several well-known Democrats were waiting in the wings.

Lane Evans was not so patient. He had started one of his shoebox files on Railsback, full of news clippings, voting records, and notes that showed dents in the congressman's armor. He felt Railsback was ignoring the district and that his vote in favor of congressional pay raises would be a significant thorn. Plus, though Railsback was married, his reputation as a ladies' man was gaining more and more attention in the district.

Lane believed Railsback could be taken down in an off-year election, when turnout is lower than a presidential year. In January of 1981 he approached Rock Island County Democratic Party chairman John Gianulis and asked him, "What do I have to do to run for Congress?"

John G (as he was commonly called) felt Lane was very bright and likable, and that the athletic young man would bring a fresh face to local politics. He introduced him to a powerful attorney and Democratic state central committee representative, Stewart Winstein, who was equally impressed by the young man. They both felt that Lane could be groomed for a future run, so they decided to let him skin-his-knees against Railsback and then later a more formidable candidate could run when the time was right.

With the approval of the local Democratic leadership (but with none of their financial support), Lane set his plan in action. His father Lee and Phil Hare went to a local bank and borrowed ten thousand dollars to kickstart the campaign. Both families put their homes up as collateral.

It was May 18, 1981. Lane was dressed in an Austin Reed suit made at the Seaford Clothing factory in Rock Island, where he stood in the parking lot and spoke before a handful of union workers:

I am today announcing my candidacy for the Democratic nomination for Congress from the Nineteenth Congressional District. Since January of this year, the Republican Party has poised itself as the butcher in the meat market. In what amounts to be an all-out attack on the social consensus in this country, hundreds of federal programs for the underprivileged, the elderly, minorities and those in need have been placed on the chopping block...

I have a different view of how a United States Representative from this district ought to conduct the public's business. I would seek to be an active advocate for the people of this district. I believe that government fraud and waste should be eliminated wherever it exists. However, I cannot and will not be a party to the reduction and elimination of programs that were established to help people in time of need...

In the months to come, I hope to emerge as a known quantity, as one individual who has gone from farm to factory, from public housing to nursing homes, down main streets and country blacktops, taking the pulse of this part of western Illinois. I plan to meet as many people as humanly possible to share our ideas, hopes and concerns about the future of this great country...

As I begin my campaign, let me make one pledge above all others: when I am elected, the seniors who have built this country, the veterans who have served this country, and everyone struggling to make a living in this country, will not have to stand alone, because they will have a representative in the Congress of the United States in Washington to stand up for them. Thank you very much for coming, and I hope to see all of you again in the months to come.

Though his words were genuine, Lane's speaking style was clunky and offbeat. The only thing that saved him was his boyish charm and from-the-gut honesty. People in the crowd just "liked" him.

"He wasn't a fire-and-brimstone, dynamic speaker," said labor leader Jerry Messer. "But you knew when he was talking it was coming straight from his heart."

Mike Malmstrom recalled: "The first time I saw Lane speak, I said 'You think *this* is gonna be our next congressman? I've heard horses talk better.'"

Lane and Phil immediately hit the road, giving speeches at every nursing home, labor hall and factory in the district, sometimes in front of crowds of fewer than ten people. Phil would stand in the back of the room and give hand signals to Lane to let him know if he needed to speak louder, slower, or change the subject. They hit the Painters, Steel Workers, Plumbers, and AFL-CIO union halls. They even showed up at grocery stores and county fairs. The unions were giving him vocal support and a small donation, but they didn't fully commit to him financially at first, for fear of losing what little influence they had with Railsback.

So, Lane's small band of volunteers made money any way they could. Phil's wife Becky, union-men Craig Wonderlich and Dave Bybee, and Lane's parents and brothers held garage sales, bake sales, paper drives, and even collected aluminum cans to be recycled. One penny, one dollar, one vote at a time, they believed it would all add-up.

The campaign office was in the basement of the Community Services Legal Clinic, a pro bono law office that Lane had opened in Rock Island, with former coworkers from Prairie State, Jean Becker and Dennis Buchmeyer. It had no windows and no air-conditioning. They called it "The Bunker." It was equipped with a couple phones and a few tables and chairs. Becky Hare acted as office manager. Volunteers delivered mail themselves because the office couldn't afford stamps. It was a tightly organized but poorly funded grassroots campaign.

Phil was the labor coordinator, Lane's brother Doyle wrote speeches, his brother Dave was the campaign driver, and his brother Steve let guests stay at his house, while friends Dave and Craig were in charge of special events. Their research department consisted of Lane's shoeboxes of voting records and newspaper clippings. They would often set up tables outside of the Watchtower Plaza, a major retail center in Rock Island, to gain signatures and small donations. A hog roast was one of their major fundraisers, where sandwiches were two dollars and you could get a bottomless beer for five dollars.

"The first campaign was really the best one. That's as grassroots as you're ever going to get in politics," Phil said. And though his support was small, and he had little name recognition, Lane still believed he could win. Then after the March primaries, a lot of other people started believing too.

Illinois has a very early primary season. Candidates have to file their collected signatures and primary packets in December, with primaries three months later in March, and then general elections eight months later in November. It requires extensive foresight and planning, and any surprises can upset a campaign quickly.

A hardcore conservative named Ken McMillan was facing off with Railsback in the Republican primary. McMillan was a bachelor, sheep farmer, and Illinois state Senator from Bureau County. This was the first time Railsback had been challenged in a primary, and in early polling McMillan trailed by forty percentage points. This did not dissuade McMillan. He believed that with the heavy support of farmers and the rural community he could dethrone the longtime congressman. McMillan's campaign focused on these rural areas and received a lot of volunteer support from the Farm Bureau and other conservative groups.

On the campaign trail and in debates, McMillan pounced on Railsback's limited support of President Reagan, saying the congressman was too liberal. It struck a chord with voters, especially in the early 1980s when the ultra-conservatives were ascending in the party and moderates like Railsback were falling out of favor.

Lane saw the rift in the Republican Party and used it to his advantage. "Lane announced that he'd take a cut in pay and that made the headlines," Doyle recalled. "He had an instinct for coming across as being real and knowing what really mattered to people."

Railsback's vote to impeach Nixon continued to plague him, as did a year-old sex-scandal coming back into the headlines. In March of 1981, *The (Delaware) News Journal* reported that Railsback stayed at a condo with lobbyist Paula Parkinson during a golf trip to Palm

Beach, Florida in January of 1980, along with two other politicians, Rep. Tom Evans (R–DE) and Sen. Dan Quayle (R–IN). Parkinson was a voluptuous blonde who appeared in *Playboy* and later became an insurance lobbyist with her husband Hank. She arrived at the condo the day after Railsback and stayed for several days without her husband. All three politicians ended up voting against the Crop Insurance Act of 1980, which Parkinson and her insurance interests had also opposed.

This article sparked a flurry of attention from the media. Railsback said he "regretted his association with her," while Senator Quayle said he was only there to play golf. Quayle's wife Marilyn said that "anybody who knows Dan Quayle, knows he'd rather play golf than have sex any day."

Railsback quickly arranged interviews with all local media outlets on March 7, 1981 and said it was "guilt by association." He told the *Quad-City Times* that Parkinson didn't affect his vote against the Crop Insurance Bill: "Miss Parkinson couldn't lobby her way out of a paper bag. I never touched the woman. She never offered us anything...I avoided that woman like the plague."

Parkinson countered, saying that she had met Railsback back in September of 1979, had dinner with him occasionally, and that they even went to a professional baseball game together. To that, Railsback conceded in the April 1, 1981 *Quad-City Times*: "Her recollections about me are basically accurate."

Though clearly caught in a lie about his relationship with Parkinson, there was no evidence that he did anything legally wrong. The Justice Department dropped its investigation, citing a lack of evidence. Local Democrats felt the issue wasn't strong enough to pose a threat to Railsback, and leading Republicans stayed silent. But the public still had questions. Voters still had their suspicions. And though McMillan never addressed the issue publicly, a whisper campaign spread across the district.

On March 16, 1982 McMillan narrowly defeated Railsback in the primary: 24,147 (51 percent) to 23,068 (49 percent), which was roughly two votes per precinct. In Rock Island County, Railsback beat McMillan 7529 to 3301. It was, after all, the rural counties that gave McMillan the win.

Was it the vote against Nixon? The Parkinson scandal? One of the other politicians in the scandal, Rep. Thomas Evans, also lost his fourth-term reelection bid. Only Senator Quayle was lucky enough to escape unscathed, winning his election two years later, and subsequently becoming Vice President under George H.W. Bush.

Lane and his campaign staff believed the upset was due to Railsback's lackadaisical attitude toward the district. "Railsback was notorious as a womanizer. It was common knowledge that he got around, so that wasn't the reason," Dennis said. "Railsback was lazy. He wasn't going out and meeting new constituents after the redistricting. Lane saw it coming."

Immediately, the dynamics of the November general election changed. The sacrificial lamb had become a viable candidate and the local money came pouring in. The national Democratic Party and PACs were still unenthused, given the fact that Lane was down by double-digits in early polling, while local Democrats and unions were energized. The Hare and Evans families were able to pay off their ten thousand dollar home loan.

The local Democratic heavy-hitters, John G and Stewart Winstein, were able to fill Evans' campaign coffers without having to report where the money originated. There were very few campaign finance laws at the time and the two men rallied every deep-pocketed Democrat in the county, along with several moderate Republicans who were turned off by McMillan's ultraconservative platform. Their goal was to maintain Rock Island County's influence on the western Illinois congressional seat.

John G and Winstein had been building up the party since the late 1950s. John G had started as a precinct committeeman and ascended to chairman of the Rock Island County Democrats in the late 1960s. They dreamt of creating a political dynasty and did everything they could to make it happen. Local bigwig Clarence Darrow's Illinois state Senate victory in 1974 was the party's first major victory and over time they would reach a point where Democrats held nearly every electable position in the county.

"My father did a big push so Rock Island would not lose its position as the home county of the U.S. congressman," Stewart's son Art Winstein recalled. "They realized they had to elect Lane Evans or they were going to lose to a downstate Republican who could energize the Republican Party around here."

John G and Winstein made calls to help boost Lane's campaign staff, reaching out to groups like the Illinois Public Action Council. One of its members was Jan Schakowsky, who would later become a U.S. Representative for Chicago and one of Lane's closest allies.

"I led a media tour of the district and brought some seniors with me and talked about why Lane was so great," Schakowsky recalled. "We went to all these different radio places. We did TV. A whole media tour of the district for Lane."

Also joining the team was Rahm Emanuel, who would later become President Barack Obama's first Chief of Staff. "Rahm started campaigning for Lane that summer right out of college," recalled former Evans' staffer Doug House. "He was highly educated and did a lot of volunteer work. He knew we were a targeted race, so he wanted to help out." Lane felt that Rahm brought a certain level of tenacity to the campaign. He also liked to make fun of Rahm's penchant for Perrier, which contrasted starkly with his tough-guy persona.

The staff began to fill out, including Lane's old college friend John Ayers, who quit a very good management job at the *Chicago Tribune* to work for him as campaign fundraiser. They also brought in Paul Tully as senior consultant and Debbie Adams as campaign manager. Adams was just twenty-nine years old at the time but had worked on the Jimmy Carter and Ted Kennedy presidential campaigns. Tully was head of The Campaign Group of Philadelphia and had over forty state and national elections under his belt.

Adams brought on a professional campaign scheduler and script writers, and formed a policy committee. She also reached out to the local newspapers; four out of five were still undecided in their endorsement. She had a strong, vocal personality (much like Lane's mother) and was therefore able to garner attention for the soft-spoken Lane. Meanwhile, Ayers urged his former co-worker at the *Chicago Tribune*, David Axelrod, to write a piece on Lane. "Our first meeting was in the newsroom," Axelrod recalled. "I did the interview grudgingly. Ayers was on my back to see him. I did it more out of a sense of obligation than that guy was gonna be something."

Axelrod was quickly impressed however: "I found him completely engaging, he wasn't like a huckster or self-promoter. He was clearly an idealist. But I also thought it was sort of a tilting at windmills escapade on his part, given the history of his district. I was struck by what a gentle, yet determined soul he was. Clearly motivated by a desire to help people. I was taken by him but didn't take him seriously as a candidate until later."

The campaign also recruited a menagerie of volunteers including out-of-work union members, college students, and members of the NAACP. They made phone calls, passed out literature, and registered four thousand voters. Lane treated them all as family, with many staying with his brother Steve or at his parents' house.

"Young people were the core of his volunteering," Rep. Jan Schakowsky recalled. "Lane would come over after work to The Bunker and thank them. He was grateful to all these students that were working day-and-night for his campaign. I remember going there and cleaning and cooking for them once in a while. I'd tell Lane that maybe we shouldn't spend so much time with them; that it might not look so good since God knows what they were smoking. But Lane didn't care, he enjoyed relaxing and hanging out with the volunteers."

Each morning when Lane visited The Bunker, he would blast the *Marine's Hymn* on the small boombox, and rally his troops. Though it was usually a room full of liberals and college kids, they were all inspired by the song, as well as by Lane's own work ethic. He would work by their side, dialing phones and passing out literature at county fairs, shopping centers and grocery stores, many times introducing himself to people for the first time. He kept an exhausting schedule. In a single swing, he traveled hundreds of miles visiting all the counties.

Several big names stumped for Lane including John Glenn, Walter Mondale, Gary Hart, and bow-tie-wearing Senator Paul Simon from Illinois. When Lane first met Simon he was a bit put-off by the Senator, who had said that he didn't think Lane was tough enough for the job. To that, Lane confided in his staff, "*Paul Simon* said *I* wasn't tough enough?"

Perhaps the most notable people stumping for Lane were a surprise to everyone: Tom Railsback's wife and his three daughters. They did a three-city airplane tour where they touted Lane's ethics and character, thus sending a lot of moderate Republicans to the young Democrat.

"The first time he had a debate with McMillan, Lane was nervous, but still he came off as more likable. Ken looked like a Washington guy," John Ayers recalled. "Lane was more empathetic and passionate and made a very strong case against the Reagan policies that were bringing the district down. He was also able to play up his local pride. He talked about going to Augie and Alleman and how much he loved Harris Pizza and all that hokey stuff. People really played into his humor and wit."

Lane's camp also liked to play mind-games with McMillan, harkening back to the Merry Pranksters of the 1960s. The two candidates would often appear on a local public-affairs show on WHBF. "I noticed that every time we went to WHBF it was freezing," Doyle recalled. "Every time that McMillan would go on he would wear this same outfit: herringbone jacket, V-neck sweater and tie. So, I said to Dennis, Kuper and Ayers, 'Ok, we all need to wear this outfit' and we all did," Doyle laughed. "And sure enough he's wearing the same thing. He didn't say a word, but he was flustered and we knew we got into his head."

On TV and in person, voters and reporters got to hear the differences between the candidates firsthand. McMillan supported deregulation of fossil fuels, aid to El Salvador, an expansion of the Defense Department budget, and was against the Equal Rights Amendment. Lane, of course, held a contrary view on all of these issues and railed against Reaganomics.

It truly was a race between an ultraconservative and an ultraliberal, with Reagan as the fulcrum.

Both candidates tried to be the hero of the common-man, but only Lane was the true populist. That's a story that's been played many times over in the Quad Cities, which John Ayers summed up best: "If you look at the history of populism, it's about class-distinction. The ruling class gaining power and money at the expense of the working class. One of the places in America where those class divisions and rivalries are most stark is the Quad Cities, because of the long-standing labor battles related to organizing at Deere and other plants. There you have particularly radical unions and particularly resistant management. The fights were very fierce there. That had an effect on Lane. It gave him class consciousness as a working-class kid."

Lane received some major newspaper endorsements, including the *Chicago Tribune*, the (Galesburg) *Register-Mail*, and his hometown *Rock Island Argus*. The September jobs report was also released and the U.S. unemployment rate had surpassed ten percent for the first time since 1940 which bolstered Lane's anti-Reaganomics message.

By Election Day the money was gone and the messages had been delivered. McMillan had outspent Lane $280,000 to $200,000. Lane's campaign rented a suite at the Sheraton Hotel in downtown Rock Island for the election night party that was large enough for about twenty people. They didn't know Lane had invited all the church congregations from the poor-end of Rock Island, nor every labor hall in the Quad Cities, so soon the suite was overflowing. Lane's staff talked to the hotel management and convinced them to open an empty storefront on the first floor, and they moved the party there. The staff all chipped in and bought more beer and pizza, and set up a single television in the corner.

Dennis was in The Bunker working phones and fielding the results while Lane stayed in a private hotel room with his family and close friends. Downstairs the party continued to grow as people drove in from across the district: union workers, the elderly, minorities, business people—a menagerie from all walks of life.

The first televised reports showed McMillan with the lead as the rural areas were reporting quickly, with county after county going to the Republican. Lane's supporters were disheartened, so he made a brief appearance at the party, telling them to keep the faith and be patient. And sure enough, a couple of hours later the results from Rock Island County were reported. Lane had won the county 33,397 to 20,109, a 13,828-vote margin. It was enough to overcome nearly every other county in the district.

At 2 a.m., McMillan conceded. It was now a victory party! Lane put the finishing touches on his acceptance speech and headed to the elevator. The moment he stepped through the doors he was greeted by a deafening roar. He shouldered his way through the hundreds of supporters, shaking hands, hugging, and reveling in the moment. He finally made his way to the podium and said: "I humbly accept this victory which the people of the 17th congressional district have given me."

"That was a campaign where I had all the glory," Lane recalled. "But I was unprepared for the attention. I knew I was gonna win, I downplayed it, but most projections said I would win. I had a gut feeling too. I knew it could be done. Ordinary people were coming out and were attracted to my efforts, and new people came out. The economy helped. Blue-collar people really turned out. I was most afraid of the upcoming second race. That's the one that really mattered."

The election night party went on until four in the morning. He shook hands with every single person who attended until the room was empty. And Lane didn't sleep. The next morning, he was out in front of all the manufacturing plants shaking hands and thanking all the workers. "That amazed a lot of them," Craig said. "He went to John Deere Harvester in East Moline, then John Deere Planter in Moline. Then the old Farmall plant."

Evans thanked each and every worker he could. He remembered one of the last men to shake his hand had said, "Good work on the campaign."

To that Lane replied, "Thank you. But now the work really begins."

Chapter Seven

Tomorrow Never Knows

Spring 2003: It was five years before I'd start working on Lane's biography, and I was the owner of a small cinema-pub in downtown Rock Island called the Brew & View. It was a former glass blowing studio with brick walls, wooden floors, and an ancient 35mm projector that ran on spit and sweat. We showed independent films and had midnight showings of pulp movies. Basically, it was the perfect eccentric spot for a Lane Evans fundraiser.

Lane's 2004 reelection office was directly across the street, and his staff would occasionally come over for drinks after work. Sometimes when Lane was in town, his assistant Mike Halpin would bring him in to see a movie (usually fifteen minutes late). Halpin was taller than Lane and just out of college. He seemed to always be smiling, always wearing the same blue suit, and always at Lane's side.

They'd watch about half the movie and then come out to the lobby and visit with the rest of the staff. Lane would sip a Diet Coke while I bent his ear. I rattled non-stop like a typical fan-boy and he always listened politely.

One night, Lane's staffers Teresa Kurtenbach, MaryAnn Floyd (Halpin's future wife), and Jeremiah Posedel came in and asked me to host a fundraiser that spring. I agreed of course.

We held it on Friday, April 11, 2003. My place only held about seventy people and it quickly filled with union men, council members, liberals and lawyers. We opened the doors between the theater and lobby and let people mingle while *Primary Colors* played in the background. People snacked on squares of pizza and sipped their drinks as we waited for Lane to arrive. I asked one of his staffers what time he'd be there, and she told me the congressman was touring the district with a state senator and they were running late.

What? Lane was bringing another politician?! This was the first I'd heard of it. I didn't know this guy. Never even heard of him...Barack

Obama? How do you even pronounce that?! If some politician was going to be speaking at my establishment, I wanted to know what his opinions were first.

But the wheels were in motion. There was nothing I could do. I had to trust them.

The visit was part of an introductory tour in which Lane could decide who he would endorse in the 2004 U.S. Senate primary, almost a year later in March. Eight candidates were running: Vic Roberts, Joyce Washington, Nancy Skinner, Maria Pappas, Gery Chico, Barack Obama, and the two leading contenders, millionaire Blair Hull and Illinois Comptroller Dan Hynes.

"Before we did this trip, Lane didn't know any of the candidates that well. So, we invited each candidate to do a tour of the district," recalled Posedel, Lane's Political Director. "Only three candidates took us up on the offer. Chico, Hull and Obama was last."

For Obama's leg of the tour, Lane, Posedel and Halpin had met Obama and his campaign manager, Dan Shomon, in Macomb, Illinois.

"We drove down from Chicago in the morning," Shomon recalled. "Barack got in the car with Lane and I remember the first thing Lane said was, 'Screw the political stuff, what kind of music do you like?'"

The two men hit it off right away. They traveled along the backroads of Illinois from Macomb to Canton, then Galesburg to the Quad Cities. They talked about The Beatles, basketball and the upcoming Presidential election. At the time, Lane was supporting Dick Gephardt, but Halpin was trying to push him toward Howard Dean. Obama said that he didn't think a small-time governor from Vermont could ever make it. Halpin interjected, "A wise man said just a little bit ago that it doesn't matter how old you are, what your name is, or where you come from."

Obama laughed and said, "I think he's teasing me a little bit, Lane."

Around dusk they finally arrived at the Brew & View. The crowd had dwindled a bit due to their tardiness. The candidates quickly worked the room and then sat down for a drink. Lane had a Diet Coke and Obama had a water. Lane was the main attraction; that is, until Obama spoke.

He had no stage nor microphone and stood among thirty or so people in the lobby. He started with jokes about his "funny name" and then segued into his progressive vision for America.

He spoke of Unity, Liberty, Hope and Change. It was mesmerizing. Everyone was silent, staggered by his poetic message. I had literally never seen such political eloquence. When it was over, we gave him an ovation that seemed to last for hours. Obama went around shaking hands and posing for photos. There wasn't a media figure in sight.

Obama left shortly after, like a comedian leaving stage on a high note. Lane watched it all from his seat, smiling with pride. Halpin took Lane home once the last attendee left. Just like in the old days, he stayed to personally thank everyone that came. My employees and I started cleaning the theater, still energized by Obama's speech. We all said: "That guy should be president." Followed by: "But the rednecks will call him Osama, he doesn't have a chance."

Lane obviously felt otherwise.

"Lane loved him," Posedel recalled. "After Obama left, he asked what we thought. I told him I liked him, but it was going to be a tough race, and if we endorsed him it would piss off a lot of folks."

Especially Illinois Comptroller Dan Hynes, who had been lobbying hard for Lane's endorsement. Hynes was a pointy-faced overachiever with a perfect part in his hair who felt entitled to the job. He declined Lane's tour invitation, and instead he pushed for a closed-door meeting a few weeks earlier. According to aides close to Lane, Hynes and his crew demanded to speak with Lane alone. Hyne's camp felt they could bully the aging congressman into an endorsement. They were wrong.

But even Lane's closest allies were leaning toward Hynes. Phil Hare argued Hynes was the safe, advantageous choice. After all, Hynes had the support of most Illinois unions, along with the powerful Daley family and over one hundred elected officials including the imperious Speaker of the Illinois House, Mike Madigan.

Lane asked Phil to wait and make up his mind after he met Obama during the introductory tour. "The first time I met Obama was at your theater," Phil recalled. "Lane calls me up and says, 'You gotta come meet this guy.' I just had a heart stent but I went anyway."

Phil was impressed of course. He even held a private Obama fundraiser in his home. But Phil was still leery of a public endorsement, especially with the Illinois Democratic establishment recommending otherwise. Lane told Phil: "This is still a democracy, I'll endorse who I want to!"

And he did. Lane held a press conference and endorsed Obama, giving him instant credibility throughout Illinois.

"Lane demonstrated his tremendous political instincts and his gut feeling for the people he represented and served," said Dennis King. "He was open-minded and wanted the best candidate. He was most impressed with Obama. Their political philosophies were so similar. So Lane endorsed him and didn't pull punches."

Dennis recalled: "We were having a discussion with Rahm Emanuel and even he said he thought we were making a big mistake. Everyone felt the same way. Hynes had the establishment. Hull had the millions. How's this guy with a funny name gonna break through?"

"The endorsement sent a signal that this guy had crossover potential," John Kuper said. "You couldn't just pigeonhole him as the 'black candidate.' Here was a guy who, because of Lane's support, could campaign downstate and perhaps attract support in smaller towns. It really opened a lot of eyes."

Jim Hightower said that it helped Obama become more confident in the down-state conservative areas: "A lot of politicking is getting comfortable. Feeling OK about going into places. You gotta campaign all over this huge state and some areas are very conservative. You have to learn how to talk. Obama had that innate ability but it helped him practice. It gave him a sense of comfort."

There were a handful of local supporters, including long-time Illinois State Senator Denny Jacobs, who was a poker buddy of Obama's: "We'd play a little bit of everything: Five-card draw, seven-card stud, hi-low. You could win or lose a couple hundred. Barack was good. He played his cards close to his chest, which is how he operates politically. He doesn't really let people into his inner thoughts. Normally he didn't bluff, but when he did bluff, he'd win because no one thought he was bluffing."

Jacobs and a handful of other state senators also gave their endorsement to Obama. But these men were clearly in the minority. Rock Island County officials were behind Hynes.

"A lot of people were unhappy with Lane," said Kuper. "I was not surprised that Lane would embrace an underdog candidate who he thought had the qualities he wanted to see in a senator."

David Axelrod, Obama's future chief political strategist, said: "Obama badly needed validators and Lane really stuck his neck out. Paul Simon had lined up to endorse Barack, and then passed away in the winter before the primary. Lane lined up for Barack because he saw the same values in Obama that motivated him."

No other members of the U.S. Congress were supporting Obama. None of the Chicago liberals nor black leaders. Even the most progressive politicians hadn't endorsed him. Obama was at the bottom of a large, well-funded pack, and polling terribly.

Lane's endorsement suddenly made Obama viable to other politicians. He made it acceptable for others to follow suit. And they did: including high-profile Democratic Representatives Jan Schakowsky, Danny Davis, and Jesse Jackson Jr.

Soon, two of Illinois' strongest unions also came on board, the Illinois Federation of Teachers (IFT) and the American Federation of State, County and Municipal Employees (AFSCME). Obama was gaining momentum.

Then in the last few weeks before the primary, he got a gift. Someone released Blair Hull's divorce records, which exposed a history of
substance abuse and alleged domestic violence. Hull remained in the
race but his poll numbers dropped, while Obama's numbers jumped
over twenty points. It was now anybody's race.

Several newspapers endorsed Obama, and he launched a heavy
television blitz during the final weeks of the campaign. And since
Obama had been essentially ignored by the other candidates, he
hadn't been targeted by a series of attack ads. His fresh energy and
outsider status now contrasted perfectly with Hull and Hynes.

On March 16, 2004, Obama won the primary with nearly fif-
ty-three percent of the vote. Hynes came in second with twenty-four
percent and Hull managed just eleven percent.

"I think Lane provided Obama with something even more valuable than votes," Posedel said. "He gave Obama support when he
didn't have much. We did everything in our power to help him. Seventy-five percent of my work for Lane was helping Obama during
the summer of 2003. Lane gave Obama new credibility with Labor,
House members, county chairs and others. I also think it was a big
mental boost to Obama. It gave him traction when he didn't have
much downstate."

Leading on the Republican side was Jack Ryan, a former in-
vestment banker who had made millions and retired early to begin
teaching at a parochial school in Chicago. He was favored to win the
race, until he suddenly dropped out that summer. Like Hull, Ryan's
divorce papers were made public. He had allegedly encouraged his
ex-wife, TV actress Jeri Ryan, to have sex in front of strangers at
sex clubs in New York and Paris. Ryan dropped out, and Republican
leaders scrambled to find a replacement. They ended up recruiting
Alan Keyes, an outspoken black Republican and perennial political
candidate.

Obama won the general election with seventy percent of the vote.

January 20, 2009: It was Tuesday, January 20th and Lane was
having one of his "good days." Several of his former staffers were
gathering at a house party to watch the inauguration of President
Barack Hussein Obama.

I tagged along with Lane, Cher, and their friend Richard Brunk
to a party at the home of Karri Gelski, one of Lane's former staffers
who was currently working for Congressman Phil Hare.

We met at the Lighthouse. Lane was dressed in a fine blue suit
and a red tie. He had a U.S. flag pin on one lapel and a USMC pin on
the other. His shoes were shined, his hair was parted, and he wore
cologne.

Richard drove us in his small sedan. When we got there, he unfolded Lane from the front seat and together we walked him to the front door. Cher followed with a tray of chips and dip to share. Karri answered and we all took off our shoes in the foyer. Everything was clean, expensive, and smelled like a craft show.

We followed Karri to the basement steps. Everyone descended except for Lane and me. He stared at the stairwell as if it was the Crucible. I hooked my forearms under Lane's shoulders, and we descended one step at a time. I held nearly his entire weight, controlling him like a marionette from one step to another.

This was his grand entrance.

There was a dozen or so of Lane's former staffers and friends there, all female. Everyone gave a polite smile; their pity poorly concealed.

The basement was outfitted with darts and a pool table, a wet bar, and plush couches. Lane worked the room slowly. Each woman shook his hand as if they were at a visitation. You could feel their discomfort despite the celebratory reason for the gathering.

We set Lane in the puffy leather couch in front of the television. The furniture divided the room so his back was now to the party. Cher made him a plate of appetizers, got him a drink, and set them on a TV tray beside him.

One by one, the women came to sit on the couch beside Lane and speak to him privately. Some shouted at him as if he were deaf, while others over-enunciated to him like a child. Each one walked away with a clear sadness in their eyes.

Lane just kept sipping his drink.

On television, we watched as hundreds of thousands of people shivered on the National Mall in Washington. The cameras panned on senators and congressmen and retired politicians, most of whom surely knew Lane on a first name basis. It made me wonder where he would have been seated among them.

Many of the party-goers said: "He wouldn't be there without you Lane."

And it was true.

Obama expressed that as well.

Just a few weeks earlier, on election night November 4, 2008, Obama had invited Lane to the Hyatt Regency in Chicago for a visit.

A little after 9 p.m. they had a private meeting in a suite down the hall from the Obama family's private room. It was a quiet place where Lane's hushed voice could be heard. Cher and Erin, Lane's former girlfriend, accompanied them.

Obama sat across from Lane and held his hand, while Cher and Erin stayed in the background. Lane was having one of his "good days" and was able to speak coherently. "I'm proud of you," Lane said. "I knew you'd get here."

Obama smiled: "I've said it before, but I don't want you to forget...I wouldn't be here without you."

They talked of Obama's grandmother, who had died shortly before the election. He leaned into Lane, close and endearing. Head tilted to one side as he listened to Lane's soft words.

"I had no doubt you'd make it. No doubt you'd be where you are today."

"I'm fortunate to have a friend like you," Obama said. "I'm so thankful that you were able to make the trip to Chicago. I'll never forget you Lane. You've been with me since the beginning."

As quickly as it had started, their meeting was interrupted. A young Secret Service agent poked his head into the room just long enough to say, "Senator, we just got word that we took Florida."

The election was sealed. There would be no miracle comeback for John McCain. And in a few minutes, the media would make their announcements that Obama was the President-Elect.

Obama sat there for a moment quietly hanging his head. Then he looked up and smiled, "Wow. We did it Lane."

Lane patted his hand. Obama stood up and said, "Well, buddy, I guess I got a speech to make..."

They shook hands and said their goodbyes. Obama celebrated with his family and went on to deliver his victory speech at Grant Park. Lane, Cher, and Erin watched from the VIP area that was filled with musicians and movie stars. In his book *Believer*, David Axelrod recalled seeing Lane in the crowd: "Parkinson's disease had robbed him of his ability to walk, speak intelligibly, or serve in office, but not of his spirit or belief. So there he was in his wheelchair, braving the bedlam to be part of it. His face was a frozen mask, but as his old friend spoke to the crowd, his cheeks were moist with tears."

And now, here we were on Inauguration Day, staring at a television in a basement in Silvis, Illinois, watching Yo-Yo Ma saw at his cello and Aretha Franklin sing in her big bowed hat.

I sat in a chair caddy-corner to Lane as Obama took the oath. Obama put his hand on Lincoln's Bible and Lane's chin quivered.

Ginny Shelton, one of Lane's oldest and closest staffers, came to the couch and put a hand on Lane's shoulder, her own eyes wet with tears. I wondered if they were for joy, sadness, or a mixture of both. We all knew Lane should have been on that balcony watching his friend, not on some couch in a basement a thousand miles away.

After Obama's speech, Lane was ready to leave. He was tired. I helped him to his feet. He and Cher worked the room one last time. When they were done, Cher went upstairs to get his shoes and his coat, while Richard went outside to warm up the car. I waited at the bottom of the stairs holding the congressman by the elbow.

He looked me in the eyes, pulled his arm from my grip and clasped the railing.

"Wait a minute, Lane, we should wait for Cher," I said. He ignored me and put one foot on the step. I looked behind me. No one said a word.

"Lane, please," I pleaded, but he had already made it to the first step. I took him by the elbow, frightened. I could see the headlines: "Neglected Congressman Breaks Hip," or "Biographer Sends Evans to Hospital."

He made it to the second step, then another, and another. At the halfway mark I let him go and said: "Oorah!"

Lane smiled and pushed even harder. I could see it in his face. He wanted to say, "I am still here! I am your congressman! I am Lane Allen Evans!"

We made it to the top of the stairs. He was breathless. I patted him on the back and said, "Good job, sir."

Cher appeared in the hall. Her eyes widened and she nearly dropped his coat.

"I tried to stop him," I shrugged.

Cher let out a long, exasperated breath: "You scare me to death, buddy."

Lane gave her a wry smile. Cher knelt and put on his shoes.

We walked to the car. Richard drove us home slowly. We all were jovial, talking of the future and the past.

When we pulled up to the Lighthouse, Lane turned to me and asked: "Well, are you coming up for a beer with the boys?"

"No, sir," I laughed. "I need to get home."

He grinned and said, "Maybe next time." Cher walked him to the entrance.

I watched in admiration as he shuffled along. The man who had just witnessed his apprentice become the leader of the free world. But I knew. That today in front of all his former staff, conquering those stairs was an even greater achievement.

Chapter Eight

I Am the Walrus

On January 3, 1983, Lane was sworn into the 98th Congress of the United States as one of fifty-seven freshman Representatives. It was the middle of Reagan's first term and Democrat Tip O'Neill was Speaker of the House, where the Democrats held a majority 272 to 163. In the Senate, Republicans were in control at 55-45. Lane had entered the "Corridors of Power" as he called it, and quickly gained the nickname "Prince Valiant" for his archaic haircut and optimistic outlook.

Lane had already traveled back and forth to D.C. several times to go to workshops for freshman representatives and attend various welcome receptions. His mother, Joyce, had accompanied him, as she often did that winter. She spent her time searching for a suitable apartment for Lane and ran several errands for him. She even helped get the right-sized tuxedo for the evening receptions. Mostly, though, she was basking in her new role as the mother of a United States congressman and making sure that Lane stayed true to his upbringing. As she told the *Dispatch/Argus* in 1983, "He's just as wonderful as he seems to be, and I hope and expect that he'll keep that basic sense of himself."

That first winter Lane also met with some of his old D.C. friends so he could ask them personally to join his team. First was his brilliant, yet short-tempered, former Georgetown classmate Dennis King who agreed to be his Chief of Staff. Then he brought on John Kuper (born with a silver-spoon and a silver-tongue) to handle Media Relations. Lane also hired legislative assistants Jeff Rosenberg, Meredith McGehee and others who had experience on Capitol Hill. The rest of his team was made up of a motley crew of friends, family, and devoted campaign workers from the Quad Cities. Among them were Phil Hare as District Director, his brother Doyle as Scheduler, and Bill Gluba as the Administrative Liaison.

King would hire support staff from more than five hundred résumés they received, while Gluba hunted for suitable office space.

"We set up an office in a busy section of Moline and I went down to Galesburg and got a main street location," Gluba recalled. "Lane wanted the offices to be visible. To be right where they can see you."

Lane also purchased a "Congressvan" which they used to drive to the far reaches of the district, so each of his constituents could meet with one of his staff in person.

Back in D.C., Lane's office was on the fourth floor of the Rayburn Building. He took over the small office that Railsback had occupied. And though he had reached out to Railsback's people many times, they gave him practically nothing for the transition. As Phil recalled, "They pretty much left us a coat rack and a cardboard box of constituent files."

Lane's mother and his staff purchased used furniture and decorated the office sparsely. On one wall they hung a diploma from each of his alma maters dating back to elementary school. On another wall they hung portraits of his heroes: Fred Harris, Bobby Kennedy, Martin Luther King Jr., Jeanette Rankin (the first woman elected to Congress in 1916) and Eleanor Roosevelt. Then directly behind his desk was a poster of his favorite, John Lennon.

Lane slept in his office for months on an old green leather couch and showered in the locker room at the House gym. He'd stay in a hotel if there were important people in town or sometimes stay with friends, but the Rayburn Building was his primary bunkhouse. He got to know the names of all the janitors, elevator operators and security officers, treating everyone the same, whether they were sponsoring a bill or cleaning a toilet.

His mother Joyce had found plenty of suitable townhouses, but Lane felt it would be a waste of money. Besides, he considered the Quad Cities his home and returned there every weekend, staying at his parents' house.

"I don't live in Washington, I commute there," he told the Associated Press in 1983. "That's the way I look at it. I live in Rock Island, and I'd rather be there."

Lane also shied away from the D.C. nightlife. He was never impressed by the fat cats or the men of means. He would attend the occasional military reception or Democratic fundraiser, but he spent his free time either chatting with the guys at the Marine Corps Liaison office or playing basketball. He avoided the late-night parties and schmoozing, as he felt many of his colleagues were vain, disconnected and lacked empathy. While he was friendly with everyone, Lane was focused on one thing: to represent his constituents in Washington, not represent Washington to his constituents.

This was the foundation of Lane Evans' career. "Representation is really a two-way street," he told the *Dispatch/Argus*, "Coming home from Washington on weekends is the best way I know of keeping in touch with the people I represent. My contact with constituents, and the actions I take to make sure their concerns and problems are addressed, is the most gratifying part of my job."

Lane had given Phil just two weeks to create a constituent services program from scratch. He told Phil that it had to be responsive, with a military-level attention to detail, so that no one fell through the cracks. They used the plan that Phil created up until the day Lane retired.

First, they staffed the offices with twice the number of assistants that Railsback had, ensuring nearly every call was answered. Within forty-eight hours, that caller would receive a letter stating that Lane was on the case. Then the caseworker would send a letter to the necessary agency, such as the VA, with a cover letter from Lane Evans requesting a direct response. This ensured that the agency would reply. Then Lane's office would relay the information to the constituent whether it was good news or bad. If they weren't satisfied with the answer, and the case was justified, Lane's office would pursue it further.

"The best advice Lane gave me," Phil recalled, "Was to always look at a problem through the eyes of the person coming in here. Not how you see it. How they see it. This is the last outpost for a lot of people. No one walks out of this office feeling like they weren't heard or without some type of caring for them."

They handled 2,644 cases in his first two years in office. This included people who wanted to reenlist in the armed services but ran into roadblocks, those who were not getting their benefits from Social Security, veterans who needed to get into the VA hospitals, and even business owners who wanted to land a government contract.

"We took every call seriously. If someone wants a birthday card for their granddaughter or a flag that flew over the Capitol, or someone is dying because of Agent Orange and couldn't get compensation, we did our best to help," Phil said.

The women who answered the phones were his frontline. There to listen to the rantings, the spit, the vile and venom, all with a friendly, understanding tone in their voice. They were the first impression. There to take the flack. The verbal shrapnel. And in the same day, perhaps give a kind word or sympathy to a crying, defeated person on the other end of the line. Lane knew that these frontline warriors were more crucial to his success than any pollster, makeup artist or speech writer. They would be his voice, face and mediator in absentia.

Staffers were expected to field concerns in-person as well. As staff member Craig Wonderlich remembered, "Even if you were at a parade or a party and someone mentioned something, you were supposed to take notes and turn that in later to the office. You definitely did not want to forget to pass on something."

That's because Lane pushed his staff as hard as he pushed the bureaucracies. "I view my organization like I do the Marine Corps. It should perform. It should be there," he told the *Dispatch/Argus*. "It's got to be a fighting organization. And if you aren't willing to fight, and you aren't willing to put in long hours, it's *adios*, you've got to go. I am a very tough boss, I expect a lot, but I'm pleased that I get a lot out of my people and that they work very hard. You've got to come motivated to work for me."

One of those first workers was Ginny Shelton. A sweet, yet gritty, woman that looked like she slept on a bed of nails. She and her husband had both recently lost their jobs, so Lane hired her as an intern. Within six months she became Chief Case Worker.

"Lane took a chance on me when my husband and I had both hit rock bottom," she said. "The most important thing I can say about Lane, is that he backed you one-hundred percent. He was very supportive and always appreciative. I always just had so much respect for him. I never wanted to let him down. All of us that worked for Lane, all felt that way. He was putting in so many hours, it was nothing to work fourteen-hour days."

Joyce Bean oversaw the two-person staff at the Galesburg office, and would often come to the Moline office where they'd team up for more difficult cases. Caseworkers were assigned to specific issues, such as veterans' affairs, economic development, Social Security and Medicare. This let them become familiar with the staff at those offices and solve problems more efficiently. They handled everything from ensuring benefits compensation to helping abused women escape their situations.

Local nonprofits also called upon Lane when they were having troubles. Longtime director of Project NOW (a local social services organization) Vince Thomas, said: "He was very supportive of our programs, and we used to encourage our clients to call Lane on certain issues, especially immigration, they'd help if paperwork was being delayed."

Lane's office tried to help every individual, Democrat, Republican or nonvoter. "Service was the name of the game. We don't care what their politics are," Ginny said. "Lane's philosophy was that government should work for all people, not just people that can afford a good attorney."

On some weekends, Lane would sit at a table in front of a local grocery store so constituents could come "shake his hand, or shake their fingers at him," as he told the *Dispatch/Argus*. "I've always said that I'm pleased to represent a district not only that tells their congressman what to do, but 'where to go,' from time to time."

He made sure to visit each of the fourteen counties in his district and logged over 35,000 miles in the first year alone. He also sent out over 225,000 newsletters with questionnaires on issues. He then logged all the results.

John Kuper also made sure they were reaching out to the newspapers as much as possible: "I let everyone know how hard he was working. I would send one or two press releases per day. There was no internet yet, so I would literally write PRs and then send them by overnight mail or fax them to newsrooms. That's how we did things in the early 1980s."

Lane then reached beyond the traditional print media and did something revolutionary for a politician at the time; he started a cable access show. *Calling on Congressman Evans* was televised every Saturday night at 5:30. The phone number flashed on the screen and he'd field live calls. He was the first person in Congress to capitalize on the technology.

"He was a big cable TV advocate," Kuper said. "He used cable to reinforce his district operation in Congress. He understood that having cable was important to small-town and rural people."

Lane quickly became a celebrity even with non-voters. His old friend Terry Knoch said: "We'd be walking around town and people would yell, 'Hey that's the guy on television!' They didn't even know the issues or anything, they just recognized him from TV."

News of Lane's celebrity drew attention on Capitol Hill as well. One Memorial Day a reporter from the *Congressional Quarterly* joined Lane on a visit to the Quad Cities. Lane's former scheduler Jerry Lack recalled: "We were at the bicycle races in Moline and everyone kept coming up to him and calling him Lane. It shocked the reporter that everyone called him by his first name. He said he'd never seen anything like it and was really thrown by the fact that people weren't afraid to come up to him, or hand him a beer and a sandwich."

While Lane focused on the people and the issues, Dennis handled the staff, keeping a strict chain of command in place. "I handled the organizational side of his office like a military chief of staff. I was in charge of deploying our resources in an effective manner. This allowed Lane to go out and be a congressman."

The military-like structure of his office was important to Lane: "Everyone had a one-on-one relationship with him, but he also believed in chain of command. The interns couldn't go above me or else we'd have chaos ensue," Dennis said. "Lane attracted good people and made them feel good about what they were doing. He encouraged them, but he was very results-oriented and wanted people to be held accountable for their results and efforts. We had to make sure the entire organization was keeping the priorities of the boss."

One of Lane's first priorities in Congress was to push his populist philosophy, so he founded and chaired the House Populist Caucus along with thirteen other Democrats, including Tom Daschle, Berkley Bedell, Al Gore, Frank McCloskey, Bill Richardson, Harold Volkmer, Gerry Sikorski, Tim Penny, James Oberstar and Barbara Boxer. (Boxer's office was next door to Lane's, and the two immediately forged a close friendship. Their staff even formed a co-ed softball team called the "Boxer Rebellion." It was comprised of, as John Kuper said: "Nice looking, athletic California women, and a bunch of Midwestern guys who were way below their league.")

Populism originally took hold in the United States in the late 1880s in response to the inequalities brought about by the Gilded Age and the Panic of 1873. Average Americans were literally dying in the streets, while factory owners like Andrew Carnegie enjoyed their vacation castles in Europe. A collection of farmers and laborers in the South and Midwest organized the People's Party to enact anti-trust laws and other progressive economic reforms. Populism was meant to address the deficiencies of capitalism, as there was no safety-net for workers and most of the country's wealth was hoarded by the property owners. The Populists wanted candidates who would put the country back to work, building roads, schools and other infrastructure. They grew powerful enough to nominate presidential candidate James Weaver in 1892, as well as elect 10 Populist governors, six U.S. Senators and thirty-six members of the House. In 1896, the Populists nominated William Jennings Bryan for President and they merged into the Democratic Party. Bryan handily won the South, but the Laborers in the North voted for Republican William McKinley, who won the presidency.

Today, the term "populist" has become a blanket term for any anti-establishment candidate or someone popular with the common voter. This upsets many purists like Jim Hightower, who described Populism as: "A doctrine, history, and an organized movement to empower ordinary folks to battle the financial and corporate elites." Or in other words, "Populism is standing up for the little guys against the bankers, big-shots and bastards."

Lane's Populist caucus was going to push for a progressive tax policy, more credit access for farmers, revocation of the 1981 corporate tax cuts, and for better enforcement of antitrust laws.

"We're looking for some real old-time political scraps with the forces of reaction and unbridled corporate power," Lane told the *Dis-*

patch/Argus in 1983. "We're all card-carrying capitalists. We believe in oil companies; we just want a lot of them. The idea behind populism is to promote competition the way it's supposed to be, not huge monopolies or unfair corporate practices." Lane believed in Competitive Capitalism rather than Consolidated Capitalism.

In keeping with the populist philosophy, Lane did something practically unheard of on Capitol Hill -- he declined a $9,100 pay raise and didn't enroll in the retirement plan. He also returned ten percent of his $60,000 salary to the U.S. Treasury. It was a sign of solidarity with the people of the district, twenty thousand of whom lost their jobs during the manufacturing downturn. "My people don't get those types of perks, why should I?" he told the *Dispatch/ Argus*.

People often asked why he didn't donate that portion of his salary to local charities. Lane says he simply did not want to choose one good cause over another. Plus, he felt that giving it back to the Treasury was the best way to protest the ever-increasing debt and budget deficits.

Of course, being a bachelor obviously made it much easier for Lane to turn down perks and raises and live a frugal life. He believed that he had chosen a life of public service and that came with obvious self-sacrifice. He was called to the seminary as a youth, but still had that desire to be a pauper serving the people. And this was the way he could achieve that.

"I don't have some of the responsibilities of a family that some of these other people do, but I don't have some of the advantages either," he told the *Dispatch/Argus*. "I'm not sure what the benefits are," he laughed. "That's probably why I'm single."

But Lane was human too. And love would bite him when he least expected it.

Chapter Nine

All My Loving

Spring 2009: I thought his name was Maelstrom. It would have been fitting for the long-haired, red-bearded Norsemen who was just as fierce as a Scandinavian storm. But it was Mike Malmstrom. He rode a motorcycle adorned with military flags and led "Stand Down," a local organization that helped homeless veterans. He was two years younger than Lane, a former Marine and worked as Lane's driver from 1987 to 1993. Malmstrom was appointed Lane's co-guardian with Cher in 2007. And while she took care of Lane's medical and daily needs, he was Lane's protector and bodyguard.

I interviewed Malmstrom one morning as he mopped the floors at the American Legion in Moline. He wore a USMC t-shirt, jeans and a leather vest with silver chains that stretched tight across his beer belly. He told me about the first time he met Lane: "In 1982 before Lane was elected, we all attended the Milan Labor Day Parade. Doyle was supposed to drive him and got sick. So they asked me to drive."

After the Milan parade, Malmstrom had to get Lane to another parade in Kewanee that started in just forty-five minutes. It was a fifty-mile trip.

"I had an old mud-dauber truck with a big round sign in back that said 'Lane Evans for Congress.' We're running down the highway in this 4x4 doing eighty. People would honk and he'd wave out the window. He was like a kid in a candy store. We made it to the parade. From that day on I drove him every Labor Day."

A few years later Lane's twenty-something scheduler/driver Jerry Lack was being promoted to Economic Development Director, so they were looking for a replacement. Preferably someone young and with little responsibility. But that plan went out the window when Lane heard that Malmstrom had recently been laid off from his factory job. Lane immediately hired the middle-aged father of three.

"He was the brains and I was the brawn. He liked to call me Old

Corps. I called him corporal, because I made sergeant. 'The Little Corporal.' That was my name for him. Except in public. I always called him Congressman," Malmstrom recalled.

They spent each weekend driving from event to event around the district.

Malmstrom drove Lane in an unmarked van with civilian license plates. Lane never used congressional plates because he wanted to be incognito and didn't want any favors from the authorities. Sometimes this was tough given Malmstrom's lead-foot.

"The first time I got pulled over, I made mention that I was driving Congressman Evans," Malmstrom said. "When it was over Lane said, 'You don't do that. We'll take care of the ticket. Don't use the fact that you're driving the congressman around.'"

Over the years they accrued several tickets, and Malmstrom was on court supervision twice.

The two men didn't talk much in the van. Mostly they'd listen to music or Lane would sleep or read. Sometimes they'd joke and tell old Marine stories, but they never spoke of policy. Another thing that was strictly off limits was Lane's personal life.

"Just as I was starting as the driver, Phil wanted me to report all the details even about his off-time. But Lane liked his privacy. I learned that the hard way. One time I said something to Phil about Lane going out for coffee or something inconsequential, and Lane got wind of it and pulled me to the side and said: 'If you want to work for me, my private life stays private.' I told myself then and there that if it isn't congressional, then no one needs to know."

Lane didn't want to discuss his family, his childhood, and especially not his love life. This led to a long-held rumor that he was a homosexual, which was still taboo for a politician at the time. Political opponents pushed that rumor with whisper-campaigns and insinuations. But the average voter didn't care one way or another. And anyone who spent more than a few minutes with the man and heard his comments or watched his eyes, knew it was just a petty rumor.

"The congressman had a right to a private life," Malmstrom said. "Lane didn't have much of a private life though." Being a congressman was his main priority.

"He just worked so hard all the time," Lack said. "The constituents were his family. And really, Lane just never wanted to get married. He'd date someone for a while, and then the women would get impatient with him. They wanted him to commit."

Lane approached his job in the same way as a Catholic priest. He didn't want to get married because either the wife would suffer or his job would suffer, and it was unfair for either to be neglected.

It was also hard for him to meet people, given the formality of Washington and his celebrity in the Quad Cities. Not to mention an overprotective mother. There were few dates that met Joyce's approval. She was cordial to the women in public, but made her criticisms known in private. Even as a grown man Lane often hid women from his mother.

There was one woman that Joyce couldn't chase away though. A smart, successful idealist named Erin Saberi.

I had met Erin in April of 2009 when she came to the Quad Cities from California for a few days. She and Lane were in the cafeteria of the Lighthouse finishing their lunch. She stood and greeted me with a handshake across the table. I sat down and politely declined her offer to finish Lane's salad.

She fed Lane pie by the forkful. After each bite, he'd lean and slowly fall into her chest like a baby wanting to nurse. She'd push him upright and give him another bite. I could tell he was faking the loss of balance. The man wanted to cuddle. And I couldn't blame him. She was pretty, with thick black hair and no need for makeup. She had a soft-brown complexion and gentle tone to her voice. And I heard a LOT of that voice. From the moment I sat down she barely took a breath, asking me question after question about my life before I could even finish the previous answer. I assumed she wasn't being rude, just protective. It was still annoying though. Along with the fact that she kept calling him "Darling."

At one point an old woman came up to the table and asked to shake Lane's hand. She told him that her husband had Parkinson's too, and that Lane was an inspiration. Erin spoke on Lane's behalf; she was cordial and polite as if she'd experienced this several times before.

After Lane finished dessert, we went up to his apartment. I carried my briefcase in one hand and a tray of leftovers in the other. Erin guided Lane by the elbow.

She put Lane on the couch and sat beside him. Then he pulled his trick again, gently dropping his head onto her shoulder. She pushed him upright and propped him up with a pillow. It was then I realized Lane hadn't even said hello to me yet. From the dining room to the couch, he hadn't even acknowledged my presence!

I suddenly felt like a third wheel. I decided to make the interview quick...

Erin told me how they met: "I think it was about 1985, it was a movie premier in Georgetown. Something with Daryl Hannah in it. At the reception I went to the bar to get a glass of wine, and I saw Lane. He was getting a drink and hitting on Daryl." Erin laughed. When Daryl walked away, Erin went up to Lane and said to him,

"Do I know you? I don't know why, but I feel like I knew you." Lane thought it was a pick-up line. He stuck out his hand and declared: "Congressman Lane Evans."

After a little small talk, they immediately went to their favorite subject of politics and found a common liberal ground. Erin told him how she was upset that the U.S. was going into the business of police training in South America, a topic that Lane was completely unaware about. He gave Erin his card and asked her to call his office and set up a meeting.

"I'm thinking this is great. I'm finally getting to see a congressman," Erin said. But Lane obviously had some ulterior motives. "After the meeting he asked me to lunch. It was kind of our first date."

The two began dating almost immediately. Renting VHS movies. Listening to records. Going to concerts. Always in D.C., because Lane kept their relationship hidden from the media and his constituents. Not because he was embarrassed. He was simply dedicated to keeping his private and public life separate.

A short time into their relationship, Erin's sister Deirdre Milano moved to D.C. "Lane was the first one who picked me up at the airport by himself, in a beat-up van," Deirdre said in a later interview. "I remember the first gift he gave my sister when they were dating... It was a toaster! He was so pragmatic. My mom and sister and I were laughing about that for years. He loved giving practical things like gas cards."

Lane treated Deirdre like a little sister. She helped him with his color-blind wardrobe and he helped her pick out a car. "Lane took me to Avis and bought one of their retired cars. It was a Chevy Sprint, putt-putt car. Years later he ended up buying it from me. He drove it to work and the Capitol police wouldn't believe he was a congressman in a car like that. They would ask for his credentials because they didn't know who he was. Except the guys in the parking garage. They all knew him."

Erin recalled one of their earliest dates: "We went to see the Huey Long movie. I remember we saw this poor guy on the street and we both went to give him money at the same time. That was a metaphor, I think for our relationship..." She paused for a moment and squeezed Lane's hand. "We gave it all to everyone else instead of each other."

Erin got up and went to the kitchenette for a glass of water. I couldn't tell if she was stifling tears or not, but she didn't really seem the type. Lane was still ignoring me.

After a minute of silence Erin called from the kitchen, pointing out a juicer she had purchased. She had been making him smoothies with spinach and turmeric and all sorts of other superfoods. The extra nutrition would help with his symptoms, she said. She had also forced him to take more walks and do extra stretching. And from what I saw in those few short days, it was true. I could tell he was already more limber and his voice more powerful. He also wasn't taking all of his prescriptions.

I don't know if it was the juice, the exercise, or the absence of medications, but he was more focused than I'd seen him in months.

"Anyway, has he told you about meeting Paul McCartney?" Erin returned to the couch, smiling. "We were at some anti-landmine event. Paul McCartney was there. We see him and Lane stepped in front of me and introduced himself. Someone took a picture. In the picture he's saying to Lane, 'I used to be a Beatle, who the hell are you?' It was the first time I've ever seen him star-struck. He used to open doors for me, he'd probably even put a jacket over a mud puddle. But when we met Paul McCartney, he was a twelve-year-old boy."

I laughed. Lane smiled. He finally made eye contact with me. It was more of a glare than a grin. I'd seen that look before—the man wanted me *gone*.

I shut the lid of my laptop and stood up. "Well, I know Lane gets pretty tired after lunch, so I better get moving."

Out of nowhere she said: "Sometimes, I think that's what made him sick. The weight of the world. I told him that often. It's like the Ringo Starr song, *Weight of the World*. You know, Lane carried it on his shoulders, and it made him sick. 'Don't carry it. We're not getting any younger,'" she turned to Lane. "How's that go? 'We've all been used, we've got to lose the weight of the world, and it's taking us down.'"

He mumbled something and smiled. Then he gave me the eye again, clearly wanting me to leave. I offered my hand to Erin. "Thanks again for meeting with me. Maybe we can talk on the phone later?"

"That'd be great. I think we're going to rest now."

Lane grinned at me.

As I shut the door, I saw him slowly fall into her again.

I'd never seen him so happy.

Chapter Ten

Don't Let Me Down

"If any group of Americans is entitled to compassion and fairness from their government, it is the veterans who have fought to preserve our freedom. In many cases, these citizens have made the extreme sacrifices: separation from their homeland, from their friends and family, and the loss of their physical and emotional well-being...I don't understand how a nation can expect future sacrifices from our fighting men and women, when our present veterans are treated so disrespectfully." — Lane Evans, 1983.

In his first term, Lane won a seat on two House Committees, Agriculture and Veterans' Affairs. He coveted both seats, but his heart was in the Veterans' Affairs Committee. It was where the former Marine felt he could do the most good, since veterans' legislation could affect up to a third of the country (when including dependents). He set out to be their champion and put into practice something that he learned during Marine boot camp: "Service beyond one's self is a worthy endeavor."

One of his first endeavors was to help restore funding to veterans programs. The year before he took office, Congress had voted to cut spending on veterans programs by over five hundred million dollars over the course of three years. Lane immediately proposed that the funding be restored, and that it be included in the Mandatory Spending of the federal budget, rather than Discretionary Spending. This meant that there would be a steady stream of money, instead of being subject to the whims of appropriators.

Lane also introduced a bill that saved the popular "Veterans Center" program and added fifty-two new centers nationwide, with one of them in the Quad Cities. Veterans Centers were located in high-traffic store-fronts and offered counseling, group sessions, and crisis intervention to vets and their families, without a lot of red tape. The program was set to be phased out in late 1984, but Lane's bill successfully extended it through 1988.

Fellow Veterans' Affairs Committee member and conservative Democrat Bill Lipinski (D-IL) often battled with Lane, yet the two still formed a close friendship.

"We became friends because we came into Congress at the same time," Lipinski said. "He was a very honest sincere and hardworking individual. In the course of a career in politics, you don't meet many people with the qualities that Lane had."

"They were great friends," said Lack. "They were funny together, Bill would ask 'What's the socialist communist idea on this issue?' Then Lane would rail him about not being a true Democrat."

The two would go out to dinner and discuss issues that affected Illinois. They also talked a lot on the phone and on the House floor. They would often butt heads in the Committee but then worked together when the time called. "Philosophically, he and I were miles and miles apart," Lipinski said. "One time that we did cooperate very strongly was when the barracks were bombed..."

It would be a defining moment in both men's careers.

In September 1982, President Ronald Reagan deployed eight hundred U.S. Marines to Beirut as part of a multinational peacekeeping force following Israel's 1982 invasion of Lebanon. The Marines enforced a cease-fire between the Palestine Liberation Organization (PLO) and Israelis. There were several small attacks on the Americans during this time, including a truck bomb that killed 63 at the American Embassy. Reagan ordered warships to the coast of Lebanon in response, while Secretary of Defense Caspar Weinberger argued for a withdrawal of forces.

A year later in September of 1983, Congress voted on a resolution that would commit the Marines to another eighteen months in Lebanon. Lane was worried about the troops' safety and he took to the House floor on September 27th to speak out:

"The attitude is that we have to persevere, we have to maintain our credibility, we can't run away from this problem. But, when any of us here in this Chamber say 'we' we really mean 'they' – the 18 and 19-year-old Marines. They have to persevere. They have to fight. And if this war is anything like the last one, 'they' will be disproportionately working class, 'they' will be disproportionately black, 'they' will be disproportionately Hispanic, and 'they' will include few of our own sons or relatives. And while we are so worried about retaining our credibility in the international community, we are losing our credibility in our own country...No one has given us a clear and solid explanation of why we are there. So, while I question no Members intentions, I suggest that if you are to be consistent, if you really feel that WE have to persevere, then vote for the Resolution on Thursday. But do two more things on Friday - enlist in the Marines and volunteer for duty in Lebanon. Then, after eighteen months, maybe you can tell us why we are there."

The resolution passed. Lane was called a coward and unpatriotic even by members of his own party. But he believed the Marines in Lebanon were in imminent danger, especially those at the Beirut airport. And tragically, he was soon proven right.

On the morning of October 23, 1983, a suicide bomber detonated a truck bomb inside the Marine barracks at the Beirut Airport, killing 241 American service members and injuring sixty more. The truck had barreled through a five-foot-high barbed wire fence, through a small guard shack, and detonated inside the four-story headquarters of the 1st Battalion 8th Marines. Two minutes later, a second bomb was detonated at the nearby French barracks, killing fifty-eight. A group calling themselves "Islamic Jihad" claimed responsibility for the attack. It was later revealed that they were affiliated with Hezbollah, a militant political group with ties to Iran and Syria.

When Lane received the news back home in Rock Island, he was enraged.

"That was the angriest I ever saw him," Phil recalled. "He was so incredibly mad. I won't get into the words he used, but trust me, it was bad. He said, 'We lost 240 Marines! I've been trying to tell that caucus of ours! And the families! What do you tell the families?!'"

Lane's big brother Steve, the Vietnam vet, called him shortly after hearing the news: "You got elected to do something, so what the hell are you going to do about it?!"

Lane immediately called his legislative assistant, Meredith McGehee, and asked her to start drafting a House Resolution that called for the "prompt and orderly withdrawal" of the Marines. He then began calling colleagues to rally support and by the next morning he was back in D.C.

At noon, sixty members of the House Democrats were discussing the attacks on the House floor. Phil recalled: "Lane got up and railed against his own party for not listening to him sooner. At one point, Democratic Speaker of the House Tip O'Neill asked 'Who the hell is that?', and someone said, 'I don't know, but he's really pissed off.'"

"Our Marines were sitting ducks," Lane said later at a news conference, as reported by the *Dispatch/Argus*. "I'm sick and tired of seeing young American Marines killed without a real reason for their deaths! ... I don't know if this guy (O'Neill) [sic] ever learns. We elect him as Speaker and he tends to never listen to us... My opposition to him is widening. Sometimes I feel just as out of touch with him as I do Ronald Reagan."

O'Neill said that a withdrawal would be a victory for Syria and the Russians: "I just don't think it's a time for Americans to back down from terrorism." He also said that Lebanon was a vital component to maintaining stability in the region and protecting global oil supplies. Most House members agreed, as did some Quad City newspapers. The *Geneseo Republic* stated: "Why are some so-called leaders in Congress moaning and crying to yank our Marines out of Lebanon? Their antics and posturing for the cameras are not worthy of statesmen. They are small men in the midst of great events and they are a disgrace."

Lane was adamant: "I don't think we have a real national security purpose in being there." And at least three House members agreed, including his Blue Dog friend Bill Lipinski, Andy Jacobs (D-IN) and James Bates (D-CA). Jacobs had also been calling for the troops' withdrawal for over a month. They wrote to their colleagues:

Dear ...
Marines have always prided themselves on being the first to fight for rights and freedom. But after the Beirut Airport massacre, it is clear to us that the Marines are more like sitting ducks than fighting Marines.

And no one can tell us for what right or freedom these Marines have died.

Yesterday we introduced a resolution calling for the prompt and orderly withdrawal of U.S. troops from Lebanon. We urge you to join in sponsoring this measure, HJ Res. 395.

The resolution called for the "prompt and orderly withdrawal" of the Marines, rather than an immediate withdrawal. And requested that only personnel assigned as guards to the U.S. embassy in Lebanon remain.

Unfortunately, the bombings were quickly overshadowed in a wag-the-dog moment from President Reagan.

On October 25th, Reagan ordered over five thousand U.S. troops to invade Grenada, a small country in the southern Caribbean. Reagan had been supposedly been coordinating the invasion since mid-October, when Grenada's Prime Minister Maurice Bishop was assassinated, and hardline Communist Bernard Coard took control of the country. Coard ordered the construction of a ten thousand foot airstrip, claiming it was for commercial use, but Reagan feared it was a chess move by the Russians to gain a foothold in the Caribbean. Eight hundred American medical students from the St. George's University School of Medicine were also trapped in the country.

The Grenada invasion lasted just two days and the entire conflict was over in just a few weeks. Nineteen American soldiers died, along with fifty-nine Cubans and forty-five Grenadians. The medical students were rescued, the airstrip and a cache of weapons were destroyed, and an Interim Advisory Council was established by the United States.

It was a great success in the eyes of the American public and temporarily bolstered Reagan's popularity. All the while, Lane continued to push for the removal of Marines. The violence in Lebanon had continued and though the public had supported Reagan, they were growing tired of the conflict. By the end of 1983, an ABC poll reported fifty-seven percent of Americans supported troop withdrawal, and Democratic leadership finally took notice.

On February 1, 1984, two senior Democratic congressmen, Dante Fascell (D-FL) and Lee Hamilton (D-IN), introduced their own resolution, in which they called for the "prompt and orderly withdrawal" of the Marines from Lebanon. The wording was nearly identical to Lane's resolution. This time, Speaker Tip O'Neill urged the Democratic caucus to support it.

Less than a week later, as he was leaving for a vacation, Reagan surprised Congress by ordering the troops to leave Lebanon and redeploy to U.S. warships offshore. He also gave clearance for military commanders to begin artillery and air strikes on targets in Syria and Lebanon. All the Marines were out of Lebanon within three weeks.

To this day the decision remains a point of contention among politicians, historians, and military strategists. It may have emboldened terrorists and others praise Reagan's reevaluation of the conflict. For Lane, it was one of his proudest and earliest accomplishments, even though he, Jacobs, and Lipinski received no credit.

"I went from somebody who stuck his neck out and was criticized for having an 'un-American' stand on Lebanon to something of a prophet," he told the *Quad-City Times* in 1984. "This taught me a lot about the legislative system and how to build a coalition. It helps to be right about an issue, but it helps a lot more to have seniority."

Adding to Lane's growing fame was an article in the non-partisan, *Congressional Quarterly*, which named Lane as the number one congressional foe of President Reagan. Lane had voted in opposition to the President over ninety percent of the time, more than any other member of Congress. However, he wasn't voting *against* Reagan so much as he was voting *for* his principles.

"I don't get up every morning thinking here's another issue I can oppose the president on," he told the *Quad-City Times* in 1984. "I haven't been afraid to stand up to the president and the leadership of my own party when I think their policies are against the best interests of my constituents. These are unusual times, and I think they require an unusual advocate."

And Lane was about to see if he, the unusual advocate, had the support of his constituents. He was about to face a rematch with Republican Ken McMillan in the 1984 general election. McMillan had sidled toward the center to align himself with Reagan, as the president was enjoying a ten-point upswing in approval ratings.

Lane didn't back away from his anti-Reagan label though, as he said in his 1984 reelection announcement:

Unfortunately to President Reagan, government is inherently evil. Well, I do not believe government is inherently evil, nor do I believe it is inherently good. Government is a tool. And a tool is not good or evil. The value or danger of a tool depends on how it is used. In my opinion, government tempered with common sense can be a tool for achieving fairness and equality of opportunity. The framers of our Constitution gave us a fine set of tools, and although they are almost 200 years old, those tools can still do the job.

Lane was ready to prove that his first election was not a fluke. To do that, he once again had to play the role of challenger.

"Lane knew how to use the power of incumbency," Dennis recalled. "He didn't run his campaign like 'I'm a congressman, vote for me, I know it all.' Instead, he showed that he was angry and that he was fighting for you. He was very effective at making McMillan look like the incumbent and part of the power structure."

In his stump speeches, Lane would distance himself from the establishment: "The Congress is just as callous as the president! While it freezes the cost-of-living adjustments for the elderly, Speaker O'Neill allows a bill to be passed that raises senators' pay. This is why I feel so frustrated and angry! But I would rather be frustrated and angry than apathetic."

Lane traveled across the district in his Congressvan, just as he'd done nearly every weekend since taking office, but now he was in campaign-mode. He worked small crowds, where he was adept at recalling names and stories. He went everywhere from nursing homes to record stores, and even made a rare appearance at a golf course.

"We had this golf tournament and man, Lane hated golf!" said Phil Hare. "We're sitting there at the end of the front nine, thanking everyone for coming. And these four guys are coming in, screaming at Lane. Really ripping him," Phil laughed. "Lane was quiet. Then someone says, 'When you gonna get with the program and support Reagan!' Lane said something like, 'I'll start doing the right thing if Reagan ever does.'" Then the guy says f-you to Lane, and Lane replies, 'Why don't you just kiss my ass?' The guy didn't reply."

Lane brought in fellow Democrat Tom Harkin, who was running for the U.S. Senate in Iowa and had a pro-agriculture reputation.

Lane was trying his best to relate to the farmers, even though it took some trickery at times. "Lane tells me, Harkin is coming in, find me a farm and some farmers in forty-eight hours," Phil said. "So I got ahold of the labor halls and asked if the guys had any big overalls. One of the guys had a farm and all these laborers showed up dressed as farmers. Harkin says 'wow' and Lane tells me 'good job.' The real truth is we had only two farmers."

McMillan tried to come across as more moderate and appeal to the urban and suburban voters. He hosted a campaign stop with Elizabeth and Bob Dole, and he had a commercial that showed him flipping pancakes in a sweater. McMillan outspent Lane by a 2-1 margin, mostly with negative television ads and mailers.

The bulk of Lane's donations came from local labor unions and hundreds of small five-dollar and ten-dollar contributions. Though John Gianulis and other local Democratic bigwigs donated as well, the campaign was still on a shoestring budget. They hired a handful of campaign staffers and relied heavily on volunteers. Students would call voters, union members went door-to-door, while seniors stuffed envelopes. And to cover the most ground, Lane's brother Doyle would sometimes appear on his behalf. "We'd laugh cause everywhere McMillan went, they claimed they saw Lane even though it was actually Doyle," John Kuper said. "McMillan couldn't figure out how he was in these parts of the district at the same time!"

Just as McMillan had aligned himself with President Reagan, he tried to align Lane with the Democratic presidential candidate Walter Mondale. McMillan asked Lane in one of their few public debates: "Do you support Mondale's proposal to raise income taxes?" McMillan was trying to be clever and Lane replied, "No, Ken, I don't. I think raising taxes on working people in a recession is the wrong thing to do." McMillan paused, a bit dumbfounded, and then said: "Well, Lane, I'm glad to hear that."

"Lane was great in debates," said Kuper. "He was very fast on his feet. He was soft-spoken, so I think McMillan underestimated him. We'd prepare meticulously to anticipate everything that might come up. But in one debate the question was, 'Can you tell us one thing that Reagan has done that you agree with?' I was sitting in the audience turning white. We hadn't thought of that. Lane paused for a couple seconds and then said 'the Space Program. I'm glad they are continuing the Space Program.' I asked him how he thought of that, and he said it just came to him."

On November 6, 1984, Reagan and Lane both won in a landslide. Lane won by a thirty thousand-vote margin, 128,273 to 98,069, or 57% to 43%. Voter turnout was extremely high. Reagan had won all of the 17th District except Rock Island County. Lane won Rock Island

County and Henry County.

In his acceptance speech to over four hundred supporters at the Moline Holiday Inn, Lane said: "I humbly accept the victory from the people of the 17th. It really isn't my victory, it's yours. I will work with the House leadership and president when I can, and oppose them when I have to."

The next morning, he made the rounds to the local plants, shaking hands with workers in the rain. He felt he had silenced the doubters and critics.

"People thought 1982 was a fluke," Rep. Jan Schakowsky said. "And then, McMillan came back and he just crushed him, even though Reagan was on the ballot. The selling point about Lane and that district is that people knew this was a man of principle. And I think, that Lane proves that you attract voters when you stand for something, when you believe in something, and are sincere in those beliefs."

To Lane, his reelection in 1984 was a vindication. He felt validated. Emboldened. And set forth on a Progressive-Populist agenda that would conflict head-on with Reagan.

As one of his first actions, Lane aggressively pushed the passage of the Food Security Act of 1985. It was a massive two-billion-dollar relief package for family farms, nearly half of which were on the verge of bankruptcy. The bill passed Congress. Then it was vetoed in March 1985 by President Reagan, who had said the government could not "bail out every farmer hopelessly in debt."

Lane was livid. He called an immediate news conference and hammered the President: "When giant corporations come calling then the cupboard is open. But when help is needed by family farmers the cupboard is bare!"

The cost of the bill was less than one percent of Reagan's proposed increase in military spending, and Lane took that message to his constituents to drum up support.

"Lane could communicate the difference between family farms and agribusiness. Family farms were being swallowed up by corporate investors," Jim Hightower recalled. "Lane would say, 'Reagan is squeezing the farmer so tight, only a pigeon can put something down on a John Deere tractor.'"

For months he continued to fight for the original bill, but made little progress with his colleagues. Speaker Tip O'Neill and the other Democrats compromised with Republicans, and in December of 1985 a heavily revised Farm Bill passed and Reagan signed it into law. While it brought the necessary credit relief to farmers, Lane saw it as a failure because it did not change any of the policies that he felt led to the crisis.

"Lane never felt defeated," John Kuper said. "Reagan had implemented his policies in two years, and we were really fighting to keep Reagan from passing more bad policies that would hurt the 17th. It was hard to gain victories. We tried to just stop things from getting worse...in a sense, that was a victory."

In 1985, Lane had a near 100 percent voting record in Congress and opposed the White House 90 percent of the time. The only other Representative with a similar progressive record was Barbara Boxer from California. This earned Lane awards and accolades from the Sierra Club, Public Citizen (Ralph Nader's consumer watchdog group), trade unions, and other progressive groups.

Lane joked that his mother, Joyce, scolded him for not disagreeing with Reagan on everything because he was, in her words, "such a terrible president." Lane did not hate Reagan; he simply disagreed with nearly all of the president's policies. As he told the *Quad-City Times*: "When I think the president is right, I support him."

Lane supported arms control, limiting military intervention, helping the homeless, protecting workers' rights, and expanding health care. The polar opposite of Ronald Reagan. Lane also supported giving factory workers sixty-day notice of plant closings, compensating victims in the event of nuclear power accidents, overriding Reagan's veto of the twenty-billion-dollar Clean Water program, opposing the death penalty, funding retraining programs for unemployed workers, and most of all, limiting defense spending.

That stance on defense spending would be a balancing act for Lane his entire career. The Rock Island Arsenal is located in the 17th District and is one of the major employers for the Quad Cities. It takes up an entire island on the Mississippi River and is accessible by three bridges. It has military housing, a National Cemetery, Confederate graveyard, golf course, and several manufacturing plants.

Lane had to push his diplomatic, peacekeeping agenda, while still supporting measures that would keep the Arsenal funded and operational. Whenever he voted against any defense-related bills, his opponents accused him of abandoning the Arsenal even if the bill had no direct effect—as when Reagan proposed spending 125 million dollars on a chemical weapons program, Lane's opposition to Reagan's plan would neither help nor hurt the Arsenal, which primarily manufactured gun mounts for tanks, carriages for howitzers, and equipped armored vehicles. His votes against the defense budget as a whole did affect the Arsenal as it handled purchasing ammunition and other procurement for all branches of the military.

Local critics called him a bleeding heart. A peacenik that was ambivalent to the Quad Cities economy. But Lane was not a pacifist, nor weak in the face of conflict. His main concern was to keep young Americans out of combat and keep the number of veterans from growing. If that meant he paid a political price at home, so be it. He saw America's role as a peacekeeper rather than imperialist. He viewed the increases in defense spending as a peacetime hand-out to war profiteers. As he told the *Dispatch/Argus*: "I represent the veterans who offered their lives and their futures when their country called, not the military contractors who've grown fat on corporate welfare masquerading as national defense."

In the mid-eighties though, the Cold War was boiling through America. Russians were the villains in our movies, wrestling rings, music, and Saturday morning cartoons. The CCCP was ubiquitous with evil. While Lane's anti-war message was not nationally popu-lar, it still resonated with a lot of people in the 17th District since the economy was still in shambles.

Americans wanted good jobs and strong defense. Neither was truly out of reach because, at that time in US history, political dif-ferences were not personal. Republicans and Democrats would de-bate vigorously on the House floor and afterwards share a cocktail at a nearby bar. They would trade small talk in the elevator and dine at the same table in the cafeteria. They compromised. They were fierce without losing their civility. The good of the nation was still perceived to be paramount.

One of the most contentious issues in America was the Strategic Defense Initiative (SDI), which was popularized by President Ronald Reagan. The Ballistic Missile Defense Organization (BMDO) had been around since 1974, but Reagan rebranded it and announced it to the public in March of 1983. Its purpose was to develop land-based MX missiles that would intercept long-range ballistic missiles in mid-air. These MX missiles would be a precursor to even more advanced laser-guided missiles that would be launched via a satellite-based delivery system to defend against nuclear war with Russia. Critics and cohorts alike dubbed it the "Star Wars" program.

Reagan referred to the MX missiles as "Peacekeepers," while Lane called them a colossal waste of money. He voted against spend-ing $1.5 billion for twenty-one MX missiles, stating that they were too expensive and would needlessly aggravate the Soviets, resulting in an escalation of the arms race. He also voted to reduce overall spending in the Star Wars program from $2.5 billion to under $1 bil-lion. As he told the *Dispatch/Argus*, the program would "add nothing to our national security, but plenty to our national deficit."

Despite Lane's best efforts, the MX missiles were developed and research for the Star Wars program continued. Technology to deploy such a defense was still at least a decade or two away. The Star Wars soon disappeared from the headlines, though not from the budget.

In the 1990s President Bill Clinton continued a variation of the program with a new name, the Ballistic Missile Defense Organization (BMDO). Later it was again renamed the Missile Defense Agency under President George W. Bush.

Lane and Reagan had different philosophies of American greatness. Though Lane won some battles and lost others, he wasn't concerned about voting against the popular president. As he told the *Dispatch/Argus*: "I ran for office opposing his policies, and they'd be disappointed if I didn't follow through and do what I said I was going to do."

The election of 1986 would be a test of that theory as midterm elections are often a referendum on the sitting president's policies. Lane would take on a thirty-four-year-old Republican from Aledo, Sam McHard.

"Sam McHard was a divorce lawyer that pretended to be a farmer," said John Kuper. "His family had a farm but he didn't want to run it, so he posed as a farmer. He was very critical of Lane. It was a harsh and negative campaign."

McHard ran as if he were fighting for sole custody of the 17th District. He focused on mudslinging and accusations, and immediately pushed the perennial accusations that Democrats steal elections, think government creates jobs, and – of course – that Lane was a Socialist.

McHard's campaign aired a couple of television spots that criticized Lane for attending an event sponsored by the Democratic Socialists of America. According to *Magill*, a magazine from Ireland that did a feature on Lane: "McHard's TV adverts [sic] consisted of white text on a black background, listing the occasion on which Evans had spoken to Socialist groups. The words Socialist and Evans were picked out in yellow for emphasis and to get the essential message across to yobbos [sic] who find reading difficult. Evans found a beauty of a reply. At a debate in Galesburg, he explained that 'I am a capitalist, a card-carrying one.' Then he pointed out that McHard, a lawyer, worked for a firm which had acted against farmers in foreclosures, which is the American equivalent of smashing statues."

The accusations of being a Socialist did not stick. Lane would often reply when asked: "I'm a Roman Catholic that has visited Quaker groups, but that doesn't mean I'm a Quaker!" And conversely, Lane tried to run a positive campaign. He knew that people were concerned about the economy above all else, so Lane presented several proposals to put people to work. It appeared that McHard hoped to win simply based on negative attacks rather than proposals. In one debate Lane said to McHard: "Sam, where's your plan?" Reporters latched onto the quote, and it became a central theme in the election.

And Lane needed some free publicity. He received just five thousand dollars from the DNC, while the RNC gave McHard over fifty-two thousand dollars. The seat was a major target for the Republicans, who still felt the Quad Cities was a Republican district and they could unseat Lane with an onslaught of attack ads.

"The money kept pouring in to get him out," Lane's old friend Kevin Sullivan said. "He was the most liberal guy on the hit list, so they brought the money in, but they didn't have a candidate."

Still, Democratic Party leaders pressured Lane to be more moderate, more "electable." To that, Lane pointed to Mondale's thumping in the 1984 election in which he campaigned against the deficit, rather than traditional Democratic issues like jobs and health care. Lane stood his ground and insisted that he was the Democratic wing of the Democratic Party.

Lane won the election on November 4, 1986, with 85,442 votes to McHard's 68,101, or 56% to 44%. He beat McHard in his home county of Mercer 3,563 to 3,294.

The next morning on just two hours of sleep, Lane once again toured the plants to thank his supporters. He was at the JI Case Plant in East Moline at 6:30 a.m. shaking hands and giving high fives. "A lot of people say, you only come down before an election," he said in the *Dispatch/Argus*. "But I like to come down the day after to show them that I do appreciate what they've done to help me.'"

Lane would need their faith and support as the recession was about to get even worse.

Chapter Eleven

With a Little Help from My Friends

Summer 2009: Erin made several trips back and forth to the Quad Cities during the summer. Each visit she forced Lane to take more walks and do extra stretching. And each visit Lane was closer to being his old self – or at least as much as he could be.

This improvement in his condition would be a point of contention between Erin and Cher. Erin would tell her that Lane needed more nutrition and holistic remedies, which would send Cher on the defensive. Cher was a traditional nurse that believed in following the doctors' orders, while Erin embraced a more "California" approach, as Malmstrom called it. Neither was right nor wrong. Because from what I saw, the love and interaction from either woman was more beneficial than any pill or smoothie.

When summer ended and Erin had to return to work, she asked me to check in on Lane and to try and keep up his regimen of smoothies and extra exercise.

I told her I could visit him more often, but I wasn't about to overstep the bounds of caretaker. I was still just the documentarian; there to watch the little fawn drown. It wasn't my business to interject my opinions on his care.

Once Erin left, Lane's mind drifted again. He became less alert. Less focused. Like he had once again resigned himself to the disease.

Part of me hoped that he was confused. That he thought the whole summer was a hallucination. It would have made it all so much easier.

It seemed that my visits never truly brightened his spirits. I think he saw me as more of a nuisance than anything. Sometimes I'd find him asleep and just sit there until he woke up, looked at me, frowned and then grabbed the remote control without saying a word. There were times I wished he saw me as a hallucination too.

And yet, I still kept trying to cheer him up. To give him some stimulation or interaction beyond his daily routine and visits from the usual caretakers. Whether it was calling his old friends to ask them to stop by or bringing my children to visit, I made several attempts to break his reverie.

One Friday I brought some old copies of his campaign speeches that I read to him. And just as I'd hoped, he brightened up the minute I started reading. He even interjected with his own quips: "Wow, that's great stuff ... Whoa, that was harsh ... Did I really write that? ... Man, that was a great line."

When I finished the last speech, he said "Blah, blah, blah" and we both laughed.

"Congress is on break. I'll have more time to meet this week."

"OK, Lane. That sounds good," I said. "Are you ready for lunch?"

"The boys came over. We had pizza."

It wasn't even noon yet, but I decided not to correct him. He was referring to his childhood friends Steve Brinn and Mark Fisher. They came to see him every Friday and brought pizza, enchiladas or another of Lane's favorite foods. I'd forgotten that it was their day to visit and I usually tried to clear out before they arrived so as not to impose.

"Brinn likes to play Risk," Lane said, then mumbled something about defending Madagascar.

As if on cue, Brinn barged through the door carrying a pizza in a paper tent. He went straight to the kitchenette and ripped it open. Mark shuffled in slowly behind. He was a "Parkie" like Lane but was still able to get around without assistance. He never spoke to me and only communicated with a nod or headshake.

Brinn was short and stocky, with oversized glasses and a ball cap. He was almost always dressed in Chicago Bears attire and wore shorts in the winter. I'd often see him biking around town or driving his Subaru that was plastered with Republican bumper stickers. The man was confident and comfortable, especially around Lane. He ribbed the congressman as if they were still kids, and never shouted at him or dumbed-down his communication.

He handed Lane a plate of sausage pizza (cut into strips - Quad Cities style) and plopped into the recliner. Mark eased into the couch beside Lane and Brinn turned on the television. They were like twelve-year-olds, feeding ticker-tapes of pizza into their mouths and watching baseball. No pretense, no worries, no manners. The best sort of friendship.

It was a Friday ritual that went on for years. Other than Cher or Malmstrom, Lane had few visitors. And none with the same dedication. These were special men, who wanted nothing from him other than his friendship.

Most of all they made him happy. And for a time, Lane was back to his old self again.

Labor Day 2009: The Rock Island County Democrats hold a giant Salute to Labor cookout every Labor Day weekend at Illiniwek Park in Hampton, Illinois along the Mississippi River. It is still a must-stump for Democrats running for any local or state office, and the close proximity to Iowa means they often host early presidential candidates. There's free beer, bounce houses, and cheap chicken dinners served on flimsy disposable plates. It's an environmentalist's nightmare and you won't find any booths reserved for far-left groups. Blue-collar laborers and union members make up the majority of the crowd.

Lane attended nearly every picnic, even after his retirement. This year he was ushered in by Cher and his friend Richard Brunk. I rode my bicycle there to avoid the mile-long parking lots. Cher and Richard pushed Lane and his wheelchair through the center of the hubbub. I followed them from twenty yards behind taking notes.

For the first five minutes he was a celebrity. Old friends and colleagues all came by. They bent over and shook his hand or gave him a hug. Others simply stood back and pointed and whispered.

That year's candidates all lined up near the stage and a crowd wandered toward them. It wasn't a huge crowd like in years past. Maybe just fifteen or twenty people. Most folks stayed near the beer tent and chicken buffet. Frankly, no one was excited about the candidates. Phil Hare was running for Congress, Pat Quinn for Governor, and Alexi Giannoulias for U.S. Senate—the successor, the sloth, and the shyster, I think someone said.

Lane sat alone in his wheelchair with an expanse of grass between him and the stage. Cher was off visiting friends and Richard was caring for his grandkid. Old friend Bill Gluba came up and stayed by his side for a long while. Many people would walk nearby and nod or smile from ten feet away. I couldn't tell if they were starstruck or reverent.

Soon the candidates took the stage. Their speeches were interrupted by the high-pitched whistle of feedback from the microphone. The PA system either screeched or went completely silent. An awkward display that resonated with the crowd. Perhaps a foreshadowing of November.

Lane started looking over his shoulders, clearly looking for someone. Gluba had left his side so he was all alone. I broke my rule and went down to see what he needed. Lane whispered in my ear.

"Hold on." I jogged over to a walrus-faced man in a golf cart.

"Do you know Lane Evans?" I asked. He looked back at me dumbfounded. Almost incredulously. I then realized it was one of his old-est friends, Craig Wonderlich.

"We need to get him to the bathroom," I told him.

Craig zipped over in the golf cart. Cher saw what was happening and came over. We lifted Lane from the wheelchair to the cart, awk-wardly, like a ventriloquist putting away an oversized dummy.

"This is embarrassing," Lane whispered to me. I patted him on the back and Craig drove him to the port-a-potty.

This was Lane's last appearance at a Labor Day picnic.

October 2009: I walked in to find Lane standing in the middle of the living room, hunched over and quivering with anger. "Miserable. People want to make my life miserable."

The room had been completely rearranged.

The caretaker on duty, a younger girl, elbowed past me and said she was going outside to smoke.

"Well, I think the place feels a little bigger, Lane," I lied, trying to make him feel better. That stupid television still took up most of the room.

"That's irrelevant to this discussion," he said, his voice louder and clearer, even more than when Erin had visited. The adrenaline seemed to have temporarily cured him.

"Do you have a truck or a car?" Lane asked, walking in a tiny circle.

"I have an old truck."

"You can drive for me. This is an important job. The most im-portant thing is that you be on time."

"OK, Lane," I said, puzzled, now watching him shift from foot to foot.

"You have to be prompt and diligent. We have agendas."

Suddenly his entire body and face froze. I assumed it was a brief hallucination. I waited till it passed. Then he raised his head and looked me straight in the eyes: "I gotta get out of this place."

He went to his bedroom and stood in front of the closet.

"I have to get into something jazzier."

He was wearing chocolate-stained sweatpants. I went to the closet and reached for a dress shirt. He said *no*, and then pointed to the pile of fresh jogging suits.

Suddenly he broke into song: "Please release meeee, let me gooooo..."

He sat on the bed and I helped him get dressed, as slow as I could, figuring his mind would eventually wander and he'd forget about the spontaneous trip. We had never left the building alone together and I didn't want to be responsible for his well-being.

"You like ice cream?" he asked as I pulled on his socks.

"Not really."

He looked at me dumbfounded. Like I'd just killed his dog or something.

"Sorry, I'm just not that into sweets."

Finally, he was dressed. In a clean USMC sweat suit with black leather loafers. He held out his hands, waiting for me to help him stand.

I paused. Mentally running through every fatal scenario.

"Let's go," he said.

"I'm sorry...I'm not sure I can do this, Lane."

"Do what?"

"Well, what if something happened? What if I break you?"

He didn't respond.

"I'm sorry, Lane."

He looked at the floor.

I heard the caretaker return from her smoke.

"Well, let me think about it," I said. "I'll be right back, Lane." Then I turned and walked out. Straight to my truck. Left him there sitting on that bed. Full of frustration. Trapped and nearly alone. I imagined him screaming till he was exhausted. Red and wet. His only respite coming from the hallucinations.

All he wanted to do was escape that purgatory for ten minutes and I couldn't do it!

My guilt was nauseating. I had promised not to get involved. To not interject myself in the story. Avoid the butterfly effect and simply document the final years of his life. But I realized it was too late for that. I'd already crossed the line of objectivity. Even though I may be perceived as narcissistic, I might as well be what the man needed right now...another friend.

So, I went back the next day, half-expecting him to still be sitting on that bed, dressed and waiting to leave. He wasn't, of course. He was in his recliner watching a movie with one of his caretakers (the young guy with the hamburger belly).

"All right, Lane. Let's go."

"What?"

"Ice cream. Let's go."

He gave the best smile he could. I told the male caretaker how Cher had given permission to take Lane on a field trip. He just shrugged and changed the channel.

We walked to my old truck. I bent the six-foot congressman and pushed him into the passenger seat. Five blocks and we reached the ice cream shop. He was silent for the ride, staring out the window. I had to push him upright after every turn.

We parked. And as I started to get out, Lane didn't move.

"I want to go home," he said.

I paused. He was looking at the handful of customers inside. "How about we go through the drive-thru?"

"OK," Lane said. "But I'm low on money."

"It's all right. I got it."

"I don't want to hurt your family."

"It's OK," I said, smiling. "It's just ice cream."

I ordered him a turtle-sundae: vanilla ice cream topped with chocolate sauce, caramel, and nuts. We parked at the far end of the lot and I fed him with a long plastic spoon.

When he was done, I decided to drive him around Rock Island for a bit. Give him a tour of his old stomping ground. We drove along the river and then up the hill through the Augustana College campus. He was silent for nearly the entire time, until we passed two pretty women walking to class, and he said: "Whoa!"

We drove through the scrapbook of neighborhoods. The lot where his hangout, Lee's, once stood. The old diner, the library, and the baseball field. When we reached Alleman High School, Lane's face suddenly soured and he said: "We better get back."

"Are you sure you don't want to see your old house? We're just a couple blocks away?"

He thanked me for the "malt and the drive" and repeated that he wanted to go back to the Lighthouse.

I couldn't tell if he was getting emotional, or if he was just bored. Was he immune to the nostalgia? Or was he overwhelmed with memories? I felt a little embarrassed then, even a little patronizing. I didn't know what the man wanted to see. What he felt. Or what would bring him joy.

So, we took the short way home. I walked him upstairs and dropped him on the couch. He was asleep before I could say goodbye.

I stayed away for weeks after that. Emotionally drained, and scared that he'd again ask me to be the getaway driver.

I didn't even visit on Thanksgiving.

Veterans Day 2009: It was my first return visit and I brought along my three-year-old daughter as a buffer. He was glad to see us, and didn't mention the length of my absence. Either because his concept of time was altered, or he didn't really miss me that much.

"This is my middle child, Chloe," I said. "She's tagging along with me today."

Lane smiled: "Your daddy comes and asks me questions." Chloe grinned.

He put up his hands like a grizzly bear and growled at her.

She laughed and it fueled him.

"I'm Baldar from the planet Earth," he said in a robotic voice.

Chloe replied: "I'm a robot too."

They went back and forth like that, pretending to be robots, aliens, bears, and whatever else came to mind. Thankfully they understood each other, because no one else could have translated.

They played with his lift-chair, pretended to be starship captains, and she fed him M&M's one by one.

"We better go eat now, Lane," I said, referring to the Veterans Day breakfast they were serving downstairs. He agreed, and the caretaker on duty took him to his bedroom to get dressed. He reappeared in a collared shirt, slacks, and a USMC pin. The caretaker stayed behind, while Chloe and I walked him to the dining hall.

He was greeted with salutes and smiles. Back in his element. We sat at a table in the middle of the room and were served immediately. My toddler and the Congressman had similar table manners. At one point he held two fists of bacon while I fed him scrambled eggs.

We were interrupted several times by widows who thanked him for his service and shared stories of their husbands' time in the military. He thanked each one of them and he soon started to tear up. I asked him if they were happy tears, and he said: "Well, a lot has happened to people."

Chloe saw he was sad so she told him that she loved him.

"You love me?" he smiled. Then he sang: "Love, love me do. You know, I love you. I'll always be true."

After breakfast Chloe and Lane raced each other to the elevator. She pushed the button to the second floor. The doors closed and his face turned very serious. He held one finger in the air and proclaimed: "I stand before you today. When I ask to be our Congressman, I hope you will say, no!"

It was a perversion of one of his early reelection speeches.

Then I wondered if he meant it. Did he really regret his entire career? Or had he become delirious? Either way, I'd never find out. He raced Chloe to the apartment and went immediately to sleep. By the time he woke up, he would have forgotten the whole thing.

Chapter Twelve

Eight Days a Week

Lane now had his third election under his belt, and the policies of Ronald Reagan were repudiated in the midterms. Democrats gained control of the Senate by picking up eight seats, and they increased their majority in the House by gaining another five seats.

"The district at that time was going through a horrendous economic depression," said John Kuper. "There were unemployment figures in some communities that were up around twenty-five percent. Almost Depression-era unemployment numbers. Whole industries shutting down, stores closing, an economic catastrophe. Lane was someone who was aggressively standing up and fighting for all the working people, small-business people, vets, and others who were bearing the brunt of the economic crises. They appreciated his fight, even though he wasn't always winning against the Reagan administration."

Throughout 1986 the Quad Cities economy took a series of hits. In May, Case announced it would close their plants in Rock Island and Bettendorf, Iowa, within eighteen months, eliminating over one thousand jobs. (They did keep the plant in East Moline open, which they acquired from International Harvester in 1985.)

In the months leading up to the decision, Case had bid on several U.S. military contracts to build heavy equipment that were ultimately awarded to the lowest bidder, Italian automaker Fiat. Case was the runner-up in several of these contracts and one of these bids was just thirteen thousand more than Fiat. In April, Lane brought in Rep. Dick Gephardt for a news conference in front of Case to bring attention to the fact that 15 percent of Fiat was owned by Libya and the Colonel Muammar Gaddafi regime, a main agitator of the United States. Lane wanted the U.S. government to cut off all military contracts with Libya, or any companies that were partially owned by Arab nations that were hostile to the United States. Lane also sponsored a bill (HR 4273) with Rep. Jim Leach that would "require the

Department of Defense to exclude from consideration for contracts those firms in which a hostile foreign government or a covered foreign national owns or controls a significant interest."

The Reagan administration was simultaneously asking for sanctions against Libya while awarding them lucrative contracts. As reported by the *Dispatch/Argus*: "Evans has pushed the Defense Department officials to scrap the Fiat contract and award it to Case, citing Libya's 15% ownership. Evans believes the Reagan administration is being hypocritical by talking tough about Libya yet awarding a U.S. contract that will benefit it economically. The congressman believes the Case announcement heightens the necessity for the Evans-Leach bill, which would prohibit companies with more than 5 percent ownership by a hostile nation from receiving military contracts."

Lane argued that American defense contracts should not be given to potential enemies, especially with the economy in shambles. The Defense Department claimed that the Libyan government was not receiving any of the profits. To that, Rep. Leach told the *Dispatch/Argus*: "Anyone familiar with the structure of modern international corporations understands that slick bookkeeping cannot mask the indirect way in which these transactions profit the Gaddafi regime."

The Evans-Leach bill was unsuccessful. It died in the Armed Services committee, with the official reason being: "Unfavorable Executive Comment Received from the Department of Defense." A few months later, Fiat was once again awarded a major contract. This time it was to build crawler-tractors for the U.S. Air Force, and the second-place bid came from Deere & Company, based in Moline.

Even Lane's own family was not immune from the struggling economy. In the spring of 1986 his father, Lee, lost his job as a Rehab Construction Officer at Rock Island City Hall. He was one of four people let go due to the loss of a Community Block Grant from the federal government. It had been eliminated due to the recently-passed Gramm-Rudman Balanced Budget Act, which Lane had fought viciously against.

Gramm-Rudman was meant to reduce the deficit, as it allowed for automatic spending cuts if the President and Congress failed to reach established deficit targets. It was originally called the Gramm-Rudman-Hollings Act until the third sponsor, Senator Ernest F. Hollings (D-SC), withdrew his name because the bill was filled with "gimmicks" and did little to actually cut the deficit.

Lane scolded Democrats who voted for the measure, calling them cowards and saying the Party lacked any sort of leadership. He saw automatic cuts as a simplistic answer to a complex problem and urged Democrats to take on a more populist approach, saying, "Populism is the political antidote to Reaganism."

Of course, Lane's words did little to save his father's job. As he told the *Quad-City Times*: "Gramm-Rudman is going to mean far worse things to less advantaged people. I'm concerned about how all these program cuts are going to affect those people. My dad is an old salt from the Navy. He's been through worse and he'll get through this."

Just a few weeks later, Lane's mother also lost her job when the Hampton Township Health Clinic temporarily closed due to the budget cuts. The clinic had provided free healthcare and nutrition services to about 150 people each week.

Joyce and Lee both rebounded. Joyce worked part-time at the local nonprofit Project NOW and the Rock Island County Health Department, while Lee later went on to open his own business, the Evans Awning Company.

Lane did what he could to stop the hemorrhaging of jobs. He introduced several new locally-based initiatives to help spur economic development in the 17th District. His first endeavor was the LEAP program, or Lane Evans Action Plan, which had originally started in 1984. It was spearheaded by staffers John Kuper and Jerry Lack.

"Lane wanted to hold regular town meetings but keep the focus squarely on the key issue of jobs and the economy, rather than inviting unfocused meetings that could be hijacked by social issues," Kuper recalled. "These meetings proved very valuable in promoting Lane's visibility and responsiveness. In addition to average citizens, the meetings brought Lane into contact and cooperation with local officials and business leaders in each county—including many Republicans."

"It was totally nonpartisan," Dennis said. "The people that were invited, it didn't matter what political party they were from. It brought more than just managers and the ruling class—labor was also involved. Lane really did listen to everyone. He spent hours on end listening. He'd take notes and a lot of ideas and projects came out of these meetings."

Lane held the LEAP meetings in every county of the 17th District. He'd start by reciting a list of things he was doing to promote jobs and the economy in the area and then brainstorm with business and community leaders. His staff would then compile a LEAP report to submit to the media and act as a road map for some of his initiatives in Congress.

"The report created an agenda of items to work on in the district and Washington to create jobs and promote growth," Lack recalled. "For example, one idea was to promote contracting opportunities at the Rock Island Arsenal and Department of Defense to small businesses. Lane worked with the Chamber of Commerce and sponsored several 'Doing Business with The Federal Government' Conferences to walk businesses through the steps of competing for government contracts."

One business that took advantage of the new initiative was the one-year-old VideoData Incorporated of Moline. Co-owner Phil Cunningham had started the company in a partner's basement and was soon doing video production for the State of Colorado Corp of Engineers. "Lane was very helpful," Cunningham recalled. "That experience was very positive because we were already doing small projects for some agencies, but we then got a lot more exposure."

Lane's actions flew right in the face of the Republican argument that "government doesn't create jobs." He made it a point to show how both entities can work together for the greater good. To that end, Lane also formed a small business advisory council to help him form business-friendly initiatives, and introduced several other measures to help small businesses. Some of these included: Calling for the elimination of export tariffs and increasing import tariffs; allowing self-employed individuals to deduct 100 percent of the cost of their health insurance coverage; expanding tax credits for restaurants with tipped employees; allowing farmers to roll over the proceeds from the sale of their farms; and granting tax credits to employers who provide day care centers.

Overregulation was a main concern of small business, and Lane knew that much of this was a result of lobbying efforts of larger corporations that were trying to squash the competition. While he pushed for more regulation of the big boys, he tried to reduce the red tape facing so many smaller companies, especially in the form of a fair tax code. Lane clamored for higher taxes on the wealthy, and for corporations to pay their fair share to help decrease the deficit and boost the economy.

"As a Populist, I believe that a central problem in our country is that too much economic power is concentrated in too few hands," Lane told the *Dispatch/Argus*. "For several years, very large corporations such as General Motors and Caterpillar didn't pay a dime in taxes. Yet ninety-five percent of American families paid a higher share of their incomes in taxes than they did in ten years."

Lane called for a progressive tax rate and a "get-tough policy against tax evaders." But during the Reagan administration those were policies that gained little attention in the halls of Congress. Reagan and the Republicans were more focused on eliminating Communism from the planet, even in the small Central American countries of El Salvador and Nicaragua.

"People in my district feel the president is far more concerned with what happens in Central America than Central Illinois," Lane once said.

Lane felt that Reagan was asking for a blank check in arming anti-Communist operations across Central America. In Nicaragua, Reagan supported the right-wing Contra rebels who were attempting a coup of the left-wing dictatorship of the Sandinistas. The Contras waged a war of terror in the villages, especially where Sandinistas had a lot of support. The Sandinista government in turn arrested and slaughtered thousands of people sympathetic to the Contras.

In El Salvador, the U.S. supported the military-led government to quell a left-wing insurgency led by the five guerilla groups of the National Liberation Front (FMLN). The U.S. had been sending aid to the tiny country since the late 1970s, which helped the Salvadoran army take power under the guise of a democratically-elected government. Vigilante death squads executed civilians suspected of dissent, while the leftist guerilas carried out kidnappings and political assassinations. The United Nations estimated over seventy-five thousand people died in the conflict.

Congress believed the Soviets and Cubans were arming leftists in both El Salvador and Nicaragua, so they approved funding counter-operations in both nations during the early 1980s. Lane voted against all funding because the aid simply intensified the human rights violations. "The president's plan for increased military aid to El Salvador is a prescription for disaster. It squanders national resources that we can't afford to waste," he told the *Dispatch/Argus*. "The people of El Salvador will be no better off. On the contrary, there will be more death, destruction and misery. No amount of arms or other military aid will solve the problems; it will only make things worse."

And Lane went to witness the situation firsthand. He and several staffers traveled to El Salvador, Nicaragua, and Honduras with the assistance of the Monmouth National Guard unit in May of 1985. Two weeks earlier Reagan had implemented a trade embargo with Nicaragua to weaken the Sandinistas, and Lane's group made that a major issue of the trip.

"I was concerned he would get too out on a limb as an anti-war candidate," recalled John Kuper, who was also on the trip. "Then he did the most extraordinary thing. Before we went down there, he had me find out who distributed Deere products in Managua. So we went there and saw the distributor and he described how the embargo was ruining his business and leading to poverty and starvation in Central Nicaragua. He said the war didn't just hurt his people, it hurt people in the Quad Cities too. So then everywhere we went Lane framed it all in terms of working people. He did a Bobby Kennedy global-connection between the two and made an economic argument out of war."

The group met with religious leaders, government officials, and business owners, including a private group of capitalists called Consejo Superior de la Empresa Privada en Nicaragua (COSEP). Lane told the *Dispatch/Argus*: "The trade embargo would hurt them. Those are the people we would like to support and bolster up. They will be hurt, but not the Sandinistas." Lane also argued that Nicaragua was a major importer of John Deere tractors and other heavy equipment. The embargo would "hurt private business and drive them into the arms of the Eastern bloc and whoever else will sell to them. I don't know how many Deere tractors can sell down there, but we should sell as many as we can."

Lane's group also toured a refugee camp and several small villages. They spoke with villagers, many of whom had had their daughters kidnapped and raped by the Contras, yet were still hoping for a peaceful solution. Lane said: "Most of the people we met were not political per se. They're not even particularly supportive of the Sandinista government." They, like the people of the 17th District, just wanted peace and jobs. The Marxists and Sandinistas were the ones feeding the people, so the pro-democracy message of the U.S. and Contras failed to gain a foothold. "If we think we are winning the hearts and minds of the Nicaraguan people, we're sadly mistaken," Lane paraphrased Nixon in the *Dispatch/Argus*: "The problem is that the Communists are talking about food and shelter, and all we're talking about are the Communists."

Lane's answer was to push for the Contadora peace process. It was a set of negotiations among a group of diplomats from Venezuela, Colombia, Panama, and Mexico aimed at finding a peaceful solution to the neighboring conflicts. The group first met in 1983 and was supported by the UN Security Council and other world leaders including Reagan (at first). Negotiations proved difficult, however, and carried on for several years. The U.S. opposed the recognition of the Nicaraguan government. Then in 1986 the waters became even more muddied...

In November of 1986, the Iran-Contra affair came to light. The United States had secretly approved selling weapons to Iran in exchange for releasing hostages in Lebanon, and then used those profits to send aid to the Contras. Evidence pointed to Reagan being aware of the deal, but Lieutenant Colonel Oliver North of the National Security Council took the fall.

"The Iran-Contra scandal should have gotten (Reagan) impeached, but he got off the hook," Kuper said. "He was using right-wing, Middle East money after the U.S. had cut off funding for that war." Congress had recently passed the Boland Amendments, which restricted funding of the Contras, so the Reagan administration was seeking other ways to send them support. Oliver North had coordinated the sales to Iran and then set up a network to funnel the money to the Contras. It was unclear if Reagan had personal knowledge of the deals.

"It's just as bad if the president did *not* know about it than if he did know about it," Lane told the *Quad-City Times*.

Oliver North went to trial in 1988 and was found guilty of three felonies. He was sentenced to a three-year suspended prison term, but that sentence was vacated due to trial technicalities pointed out by the ACLU. Reagan never did face any official consequences and his popularity was relatively unscathed. Soon enough, the American public's attention moved on and the wars in Central America continued.

The results of these conflicts were extremely complicated. Some historians say that Reagan squashed the seeds of communism, while others argue he sponsored terror and installed dictatorships. Scholars have difficulty explaining the situations even with historical perspective, and in reality, the results are still being played out today.

The year 1988 was a presidential election year. Lane faced Republican William Stewart, a fifty-three-year-old attorney from Kewanee who supported Reagan's policies in Central America and believed those would continue if Vice President George Bush won the presidency. Bush and his running mate, Indiana Senator Dan Quayle, were challenged by Massachusetts Governor Michael Dukakis and his running mate, Senator Lloyd Bentsen of Texas.

The campaign between Stewart and Lane was relatively tame, with only a few attacks between the candidates. Stewart attacked Lane's decision to quit the House Committee on Agriculture, saying that he had abandoned the local agriculture community. Lane said he decided to quit so he could focus his energy on the Veterans' Affairs Committee and run for a place on the House Armed Services Committee.

Stewart campaigned on the policies of the Republican ticket and, as usual, criticized Lane for being too liberal. Lane campaigned on his accomplishments and his record of service to the district. He saw every day as a day on the campaign trail, as Chief of Staff Dennis King described: "Good governing was good campaigning as well."

Lane's campaign outspent the Stewart campaign by a margin of 3-1, which was surprising given Stewart's wealth. According to financial disclosures, Stewart owned upwards of six hundred thousand dollars in real estate and investments. Lane's income was under $137,000, with his assets including a D.C. townhouse, a home in

Rock Island, a PC and a printer.

By the election in 1988, Lane had returned over $137,762 of his salary to the government. Congress had voted to hike their pay to $89,500, but Lane continued to take just $54,500 even though he still had to pay taxes on the full salary. Lane told the *Dispatch/Argus*: "I didn't get elected to Congress to become rich. It's a lot of money, but I wasn't raised that way. I've been directed towards public service. There ought to be some sacrifice in that."

Lane was also very frugal in his office. His annual office expenditures always came in under budget. Even though he traveled back to the district each weekend, his travel expenses were still just $9,380 a year.

Lane wanted to curb political donations as well. Earlier in the year, Lane had joined forces with Representative Leach to introduce legislation that would cap political donations. It would have limited the amount of money a candidate could receive from PACs to one hundred thousand dollars, and campaign spending would be capped at four hundred thousand dollars. As Leach explained to the *Quad-City Times*: "If the trend toward more expensive races for candidates is not curbed, individuals elected to Congress will increasingly become indebted to either big business or big labor. Congress will become a legislative body where the small businessman, farmer, worker, and ordinary citizens are only secondarily represented."

Labor unions, environmental groups, and other progressive PACs contributed to Lane, but often not to the level he needed. They knew Lane was like-minded and would vote a certain way, so they only contributed when they knew he would have a tough race. "Some members of Congress were ready to cut deals to get financial support for the next campaign," recalled Dennis King. "There were lots of corporate sources down there. The doors were not opened for Lane, because he didn't do the things you need to do. He wasn't gonna compromise his principles."

An army of volunteers worked for Lane's campaign, led by Kathy Wonderlich, who said: "We couldn't give him money, so we volunteered. They were starting a computer database and I would enter things. Computers were just coming of age then. If you could type fast you'd get a computer job. We were using old IBMs. Huge things. We'd save everything at the end of the day and hope nothing went wrong!"

At this time, there weren't a lot of telemarketing and direct-mail firms, so the campaign did it themselves. Volunteers would call people throughout the district and compile their information by hand for other volunteers to enter into a computer database. "It was a lot of seniors who did the calling. Many of them didn't have anything to do. This gave them a lot of comradery," Kathy Wonderlich said. "The folks would start conversations, get into talking about issues, and draw in voters. It was just a good fun circle to be around."

Lane visited the volunteers regularly. "He'd come in and talk to every single one of them that were stuffing envelopes," Wonderlich said. "He met one-on-one with all the volunteers, so we always knew who he was."

The *Quad-City Times* endorsed Lane, and pointed out what a lot of voters believed, which was that Stewart had a lack of vision: "Stewart's biggest weakness is his seeming vagueness about why he wants to serve in Congress. When asked, for example, what his first legislative goal would be, he said it would be giving the President a line-item veto. Surely that can't be the most important thing that can be accomplished by a western Illinois congressman."

The 1988 election was a blowout, both nationally and in the 17th District. George H.W. Bush won 53 percent to 45 percent nationally, and even won Illinois, which historically went Democratic. Lane won nearly double the votes of Stewart, 132,130 to 71,560, or 65 percent to 35 percent.

Lane won based on his policies, his governing, and his service to the district. He was unapologetic about his disputes with President Reagan, and said he wouldn't change with the new president. He told the *Dispatch/Argus*: "I compliment the Bush campaign on their victory, although their campaign was not based on issues. I will work with the President when I can, but oppose him when I must."

Lane would continue with his progressive agenda and commitment to veterans. He was climbing in the ranks of the Veterans' Affairs Committee and, as he'd hoped, he won a place on the Armed Services Committee that oversaw the nation's defense budget and set policy for all four branches of the military.

He had his office running smoothly, he was popular with constituents, and Lane felt he could really start making a change.

Lane was about to hit his stride.

Chapter Thirteen

Happiness Is a Warm Gun

December 24, 2009: Christmas Eve. The television was practically rattling the door. I knocked harder than usual.

"Come in! Come in!" a woman shouted. It wasn't Cher, but the rusty voice of a nurse that I hadn't seen in weeks. She was almost in tears.

Lane was in the kitchen, hunched over with one hand locked on the seat of a stool and the other clenching the tiny woman's shoulder.

"I can't get him to move," she whimpered under his weight.

I rushed over and took him by the elbow. The woman let go and stepped away. I could barely bend his arm. He was like the Tin Man again, this time desperately in need of peace-and-quiet rather than oil.

Lane's eyes darted around until they finally locked on mine. He grinned.

"Hey Lane. Happy Christmas," I smiled. "Let's get you over to the couch."

"Ok," he breathed.

One-by-one I unlocked his fingers from the stool. Then I gently pushed against his spine to straighten him. We slowly shuffled to the living room.

He plopped onto the couch and sunk into that leather hole.

That damn television that commanded everyone's attention. No wonder he wanted to escape. No wonder he lost his mind in that kitchen. I was ready to leave after just one minute, and Lane was trapped there 24/7. I felt traitorous for putting him back on that couch.

I grabbed the remote and pressed the mute button. Then I sat beside him and dried his chin.

"I didn't know what to do with him," the woman said. "I'm glad you showed up. I've never seen him like that. He couldn't move."

Lane was trying to focus. He looked around the room, locking on things that no one else could see.

The woman talked. And talked. About Lane and food and weather and telling me how Lane was feeling and – –

Gawd I just wanted her to shut the hell up! When I asked Lane a question, she kept answering for him. Just like Cher, she would finish the man's sentences before he even tried to reply. I needed direct answers from Lane, not their interpretations.

"I tried to move him and he kept – –"

I wished she'd be quiet. Wished it deeply and truly. I let her know it with a vicious stare.

She immediately understood: "I'm gonna go downstairs for coffee."

Lane and I sat in silence then, to let him collect his thoughts. Peace and quiet. The best cure for a bad trip.

Soon he was focused again.

I asked if he was OK, and he nodded.

"I brought you something," I said, as I set a present on his lap. He clawed at it for a moment and then I opened it for him. A red fleece blanket with the USMC logo.

I draped it over his legs and he thanked me. I think his eyes got a little red.

I asked why he didn't go somewhere for the holidays. I'm sure he'd been invited places. He told me he didn't want to go anywhere, just in case his family stopped by.

We sat in silence for a bit longer. Then Lane said he wanted to go for a walk. I told him that it would just be on this floor, not some grand escape. He agreed and we set off. I let him lead, walking one pace behind. Close enough to catch him yet distant enough to give him a sense of victory.

When we got back to the room, he was out of breath. I put him on the couch and grabbed a plate of cookies and milk with a straw.

The nurse returned. She had finally calmed down. We all watched a Christmas special with the volume turned low. He seemed content.

After I left, Cher stopped by with Malmstrom, who was dressed as Santa. They shared some laughs and Cher put him to bed.

February 2010: In February 2010 John Gianulis died at the age of eighty-seven. He was the Boss Tweed of Rock Island County politics and was instrumental in Lane's first election. Along with his friend and colleague Stewart Winstein, he also played a key role in turning the county into a stronghold for Democrats. The party was so dominant in fact, that – as of 2019 – there are just a handful of Republicans holding office. If you want to win, you run as a Democrat – no matter your real politics. And that's true for nearly every electable position.

In their well-intentioned pursuit of a Democratic governance, Gianulis and Winstein created a one-party system with little-to-no oversight of its more nefarious members: One county clerk got rich by selling software he created on the public's dime, a county prosecutor got a slap on the wrist for propositioning an underage female witness, a county sheriff sexually harassed an undocumented female gym companion, and a family of state legislators passed their seats from generation to generation in legal, yet repugnant, back-room deals. Even some of its most noble members still engage in blatant nepotism or double-dip the pension system. All of this began during Lane's tenure, though the level of corruption was not as evident until late in the game, when Lane's cognitive abilities had diminished along with his influence.

On a cold, sunny day in February, I escorted Lane to John G's visitation, along with Cher and his friend Richard. Cher had dressed him in a dark suit and pinned a U.S. flag to his lapel. His blue wool trench coat was clean and his hair was smoothed with gel. He looked good, but I was worried because his mild shaking fits had recently progressed to violent convulsions. Thankfully he was alert and vocal and his tremors were muted.

Cher and Richard walked Lane into Wheelan-Pressly Funeral Home in Rock Island. As usual I followed a step behind. We maneuvered through the lobby and were immediately spotted by Phil. He rushed to Lane and took him by the elbow, ignoring the rest of our entourage. Cher, Richard and I broke formation as Phil took him through the receiving line and by the casket. Then they sat in the front row of wooden folding chairs. I found a place against the wall.

Men and women paid their respects to John G, and then to Lane. It was surreal. As though Lane were attending his own visitation. A long line of friends and colleagues lined up to shake his hand or hug him as though they were saying their final goodbye. It was a gift that few people receive, but one that I'm not sure he realized.

We stayed for about half an hour. On the way home he was chatty. Energized by the visit. He talked and laughed and said things I couldn't understand. It was so good to see him happy.

May 2010: By now most of my interviews with Lane were done, but I continued to see him at least once a week. During one visit, I found him asleep and Cher nearly in tears on the phone. She was talking with someone from American Bank who handled Lane's meager estate. They were discussing his housing options because Lane was running out of money.

It was just a year ago, in the summer of 2009, that his friends in Congress had held a fundraiser called the "Lane Evans Health Care and Assisted Living Fund." It was spearheaded by Phil Hare and Dick Durbin, and they raised nearly eighty thousand dollars. That money was almost gone.

Many people wrongly assume that congressional retirees get their salaries for life as well as free healthcare. Actually, representatives have to opt-into the pension system. And as noted earlier in this book, Lane never opted into the retirement plan nor healthcare coverage until the final years of his career so his benefits were minimal.

A man who had dedicated his entire life to serving the public, was now just another wretch in the US healthcare system.

Cher hung up the phone. Eyes red and defeated. She said that without more money, Lane might have to go to the Illinois Veterans Home in Quincy, Illinois. Three hours away.

I sat quietly for a moment. Watching Lane sleep. Thinking of how the distance would even further isolate him from his friends and loved ones. Again, I wrestled with the decision of voicing my opinion. Of interfering in the life that I was there to document rather than direct. But the man was my friend and I wanted the best for him.

"Does he really have to be in a nursing home," I asked. "Why not just put him in a cheap apartment in Rock Island?" He had a twenty-four-hour nurse on staff anyway.

Cher told me that would be nice, but he couldn't afford to have a full-time caretaker anymore, and that the bank wouldn't allow him to live without supervision. I didn't press her on specifics. She just said the bank controlled his money, the Lighthouse wouldn't work with them, and their only choice was the Quincy veterans' home.

I told her maybe it wouldn't be that bad. At least Lane would be happy to be surrounded by vets. He'd make new friends and maybe even spend some time visiting, rather than just watching television. Plus, he'd get great care and be treated like a hero. The only downside was that his spirit would be crushed, perhaps even shortening his life because he would be "in an old folks home" as he called it. And not to mention (thinking in selfish terms), it would be a three-hour drive to visit him and Cher would be out of a job.

"What about Friendship Manor? Or the Fort Armstrong? They're both in Rock Island. He'd love that. There has to be some place that would work with you because it's Lane. They'd think it was an honor to have him there. I bet they'd give a discount."

Cher said it was worth a shot. She called Malmstrom. He said go for it. And Cher started making calls.

Lane was accepted into a new retirement home in East Moline called Park Vista, just a couple miles away. They had agreed to work within Lane's budget and offered various levels of care and independence. He would be alone most of the day but an on-site nurse would check on him periodically. Cher was still going to work part-time and manage his medications and treatment, as well as just give him some company.

A month later it was moving day. A hot Saturday in June. Other than Cher, Malmstrom and me, no one else had showed up to help. So, I called my favorite tavern and put out the word. Six friends arrived in less than thirty minutes.

We stripped the entire apartment with Grinch-like efficiency. Picture frames, lamp stands and books. So many books. And that television! It took three men just to get it out the door. We carried it all, down two narrow flights of stairs in stifling heat. Sometimes we got lucky and caught the service elevator and a taste of air conditioning. It was easily one of the worst moving days I'd ever experienced, yet none of us complained.

The last thing to move was the leather couch. Lane sat on it in an empty room, looking more disoriented than ever. Cher told him it was time to go and I walked him outside. We sat on a bench as two friends maneuvered the couch into the truck. Lane seemed uncomfortable in the sun. It looked painful on his pale, clammy skin.

"Hey, I forgot to ask you. Why didn't you ever run for Senate?"

"What? Parkinson's wasn't enough?"

I laughed and watched my friends bring out the last of his knick-knacks. Soon the moving truck was filled and we all caravanned to Park Vista. His room was on the second floor and had nearly the same layout as his old apartment, but was quite a bit smaller. It had oversized trim and floorboards, and several strategically placed bannisters. The carpet was plush and the appliances were clean. Overall, it had the feeling of an old woman's house, shrunk down into a few hundred square feet.

We carried in the couch first so we could plant Lane in the air conditioning. Slowly we emptied the truck and stacked the boxes around him. Cher and Malmstrom would handle the unpacking.

When we were done, Malmstrom offered everyone beer and lunch, but we all declined. My friends said it was a privilege just to help; even the hardcore Republican. Lane shook each one of their hands and cried as he thanked them.

A week later I dropped in unannounced to be sure he was getting his regular visits from the nursing staff. It was early July 2010.

I knocked and no one answered. I didn't hear the TV. The door was unlocked, so I went inside. Lane was alone, lying on the couch with his eyes closed and quietly moaning. His hair was wild and the neck of his t-shirt was stretched. The legs of his sweatpants were pulled up over his knees. The television was muted on CNN.

The place reeked. Or he reeked. Changing diapers was the one thing I wouldn't do. I sat in the recliner, wondering when the nurse on duty would arrive.

"Hey, Lane," I said quietly.

He opened his eyes and looked at me blankly. I didn't know if he registered that I was there and, if he did, whether he even knew who I was.

He shut his eyes again and let out a slow, quivering moan. Like a prisoner in the last throes of a torture session. It was haunting. And seemed to go on forever.

His body curled into the fetal position, seemingly involuntarily, as his muscles spasmed and tightened and pulled his limbs closer and closer.

A six-foot man cinched in a ball. Lying in his own filth. On that couch. That damn leather couch. I imagined the cow skin melding with his. The cells and dermis slowly growing together. Becoming his own flesh. His veins rooting through the cushions and his tendons taut against the springs. His own body disintegrating until they had finally become one.

The spasm subsided, and he let out a sigh.

I wanted to comfort him. To put my hand on his shoulder or cover him with a blanket. But I was afraid that even the gentlest touch would spark agonizing reverberations.

He groaned again. Louder this time. A deep, guttural cry like Frankenstein's monster.

Does he need a pain pill? Do I call down to someone at the front desk? Do I call 911?

There he was, coiled and crying, and all I could do was watch.

Suddenly he went quiet. He had passed out, exhausted from the pain. I checked to be sure he was breathing and then let him sleep.

I watched and waited. An hour passed and finally someone appeared. A hulking nurse with a tray of food and pills. I told her about Lane's soiled diaper. She set the food tray down and walked over to him.

Without warning she peeled him off the couch. I could practically hear the two skins separating. She jostled him awake, lifted him upright (!) and then walked him to the bathroom.

She started removing his clothes. I quietly left.

I almost called Cher. Then I realized that this was probably something he'd experienced many times before. That Cher had probably witnessed already. And given the nurse's reaction, she had, too.

This was the reality of Parkinson's.

Chapter Fourteen

Sergeant Pepper

In the late 1980s, Washington D.C. was one of the most crime-ridden cities in the nation. It had the highest homicide rate, with nearly a murder every day. Drugs were rampant and a new, cheaper version of cocaine called Crack was permeating the city. Even the Mayor, Marion Berry, was busted smoking it in a hotel room by the FBI.

It was at this time that Lane's brother Doyle and his niece Joyce came to live with him in D.C. Lane abandoned his cheap apartment and purchased a townhouse in what was considered a safe neighborhood, close to Capitol Hill and a good elementary school for Joyce. Doyle worked a handful of jobs, starting in the congressional mailroom and then at the House doorkeeper office, and later in the congressional visitor gallery.

Together, the two men raised Joyce for a short time. Lane went to her school plays, gymnastic meets and dance recitals. He even made time for family dinners at the townhouse. As Joyce recalled: "Nearly all of my memories growing up include Lane. He was a very busy man and yet he made me feel like the most important person in the entire world."

Lane's mother, Joyce, still occasionally visited D.C., but much less than she did in his first term. The younger Joyce was Lane's new sidekick. She tagged along with him to Marine Corps parades, White House Christmas events, and veterans receptions. Lane would often pick her up on Wednesdays when school let out early, and then bring her to his office until her dad got off work. She'd play "school" with the staff while Lane held meetings or cast votes. He also took Joyce on many trips, including several trips to Disneyland.

"Sometimes the actual travel time was the best," Joyce wrote. "If it was a driving trip he would always pack a bag full of surprises. He would surprise me with a new book or game every couple of hours. It made trips so much fun."

Lane and Doyle pushed her to do well in school and helped her as much as they could: "I remember in first grade sitting at the kitchen table writing my first real report; it was on the northern fur seal. Lane sat up late with me and helped me until I got it just right. He would bring home the newest set of books or tapes to help me improve my study skills or learn Spanish. He was always pushing me to be the best that I could be."

Lane pushed the people in his offices as well, because he cared for them too. He maintained a high level of integrity and held his employees to the same standards. The offices were operated much like the Marine Corps. Not in the sense of strict protocols and harsh punishments, but rather an expectation of hard work, dedication, and honor.

"He wanted to be approachable," said Eda Robinson, who worked a variety of jobs for Lane, the foremost being Office Manager at the D.C. office. She was a kind, soft-spoken black woman with an attention to detail, and a long history of working for other U.S. Representatives. "He was a people person and didn't want a staff that is sweating bullets. It was always a good environment to work in."

She explained how Lane held all his staff meetings in a circle, like King Arthur. "It made us feel valued. Lane believed that treating you like a human being translated to better work, and affects how you treat others as well."

Lane still demanded that they do their job, however, and that they do it well. "He'd always remind us that important decisions were being made that impacted people's lives," Robinson said. "There was a theme that you were all adults. We give you your responsibilities and we expect you to fulfill that. Period. But that being said, you don't have a supervisor standing over you like it is in other offices."

When employees did make a mistake or get out of line Lane might reprimand them, but most of the time that job was left to Dennis King. The blunt, straightforward man had no reservations about doling out criticism. If there was dirty work to be done, Dennis would do it. Lane preferred everyone just fix a situation and move on.

"In the twenty-three years that I worked for him, Lane never got mad," recalled Jerry Lack. "Even when we got bad news he'd just try to figure out how to make things better."

At the end of each work week before heading back to the district, Lane would go around the offices and encourage his troops. "He would go into a room and say bye to everyone," said Robinson. "Or if someone did something special, he'd go to their desk and say great job. That goes a long way."

To blow off steam, Lane and his staff would gather for a weekly basketball game.

"When you describe them as basketball games, I'd use the term loosely," said John Kuper. "It was a cross between basketball and football."

They played in the House gym, where only members were supposed to have access, so they secretly played early in the morning or late at night. "I remember we were playing one morning and had the place to ourselves," Kuper said. "Then some congressmen showed up and Lane said, 'Don't worry, they're all my cousins.'"

They also organized games back in the Quad Cities, sometimes at the local YWCA or Tri-City Jewish Center. Former Evans staffer Doug House remembered: "Lane would foul you really hard. He was always having fun, but he'd play dirty. It was a bonding experience. We'd never talk about work, just personal attacks on someone's poor dribbling or poor abilities to shoot."

"If you didn't play basketball you were nothing," said Malmstrom. "I hated the damn game but I learned it. We played jungle rules. It got rough all right."

"Lane was competitive. He always wanted to win. Lane would foul someone and then claim it wasn't a foul," said Lack, one of the few staffers that was as tall and as fit as Lane. "He'd pretend he was Larry Bird. He was a Celtics fan and liked team ball. He'd pass the ball and work for the best shot. He always wanted to make sure he had the better team. Sometimes Phil would get mad at Lane for stacking his team."

By the mid-nineties the staff basketball games became less frequent, as sore backs and stiff muscles were more prevalent. The staff pursued other hobbies and Lane took up jogging. He would run through the National Mall at the crack of dawn, and was often joined by veterans who he had befriended at the Marine Corps Liaison Office.

The military men respected Lane. While other politicians gave lip service to Veterans, Lane was supporting them with actual action. He and his staff had set forth on a comprehensive agenda to improve the lives of veterans and their families from healthcare to housing. And many times, that meant taking on members of his own party and even his colleagues on the Veterans Affairs Committee.

In early 1989 he helped revamp the Board of Veterans' Appeals (BVA). Prior to this, any veteran who disagreed with an agency or had a claim denied had no way to appeal the decision beyond the BVA. "There was no judicial review of veterans' claims before Lane," said Dennis. "If a claim was denied, they couldn't hire a lawyer."

The BVA was known for arbitrary rulings, and veterans' support groups had fought them for decades. "Since WWI, regulations have been in place which, in effect, deny veterans the basic right to due process in their dealings with the VA," Lane told the *Dispatch/Argus* in 1988. "Social Security, federal prisoners, and illegal aliens have the right of federal court adjudication, a right not shared by veterans."

Lane had introduced a bill that would have eliminated the BVA and move veterans' appeals to the federal courts. Reagan and many bipartisan members of Congress felt that was too "drastic and unjustified." In a compromise, they recrafted the bill to keep the BVA active, but establish a special court of appeals for veterans.

Essentially, a veteran could now hire a lawyer and question an agency decision. "The Vet department never allowed for that before. That's how adversarial the Veterans committee was," said Dennis.

Lane also fought to bring VA healthcare services to the Quad Cities. At that time, veterans had to travel an hour to Iowa City for even the most basic services. Many veterans simply skipped treatment, while others had to take a day off work to travel.

Lane first sought the funding for a Quad Cities clinic in 1984, citing the proximity of the Rock Island Arsenal and large number of veterans in the area (nearly one hundred thousand). Over the next five years he had to battle the longtime Chairman of the Veterans' Affairs Committee, Sonny Montgomery (D-MS), who labeled it as a "pork" project. Lane finally rallied enough votes to get the $1.1 million facility approved in 1989. The clinic opened in 1991 and was located in Bettendorf, Iowa, outside of Lane's district but still within the Quad Cities.

"People asked why it wasn't built in Illinois," recalled Ginny Shelton, who was in charge of veterans' affairs for Lane's constituents. "Well, it was cheaper, easier, and it was still gonna help veterans. Lane was just glad we got the funds; he was not going to tell them where to put it."

The clinic provided preventative and primary care, as well as substance abuse counseling, patient education, and physical therapy. They also had an on-site X-ray machine and pharmacy. The clinic ended up serving nearly thirty thousand visitors in its first year.

In 1990 Lane was honored as the Illinois Legislator of the Year by the Illinois State Council of Vietnam Veterans. He was also featured on the cover of the May 1990 issue of U.S. Veterans Magazine. The nationwide publication labeled him as the "most outspoken advocate for Vietnam Vets in the House." He was also awarded the very first annual President's Award by the Vietnam Veterans of America for outstanding achievements.

This did not make him complacent though. He felt there was much more to achieve, specifically with the horrors of Agent Orange.

He wanted medical funding for veterans and their children who suffered from spina bifida and other illnesses that many scientists were starting to link to Agent Orange. Not to mention, a war was brewing in Iraq.

Before tackling all of this though, Lane would first have to face off against Republican challenger Dan Lee in November of 1990.

On paper, Lee was a formidable opponent. He was married with one daughter, and was a Navy veteran and longtime professor of Ethics at Augustana College. Independent voters liked his moderate Republican viewpoints, while many in the media compared him to former Congressman Tom Railsback. He even received the endorsement of the Chicago Tribune, which opined that Lane was getting too liberal and comfortable in D.C.

Early polling had Lee within five points. He hired a high-profile, out-of-state campaign team while Lane handed the reins to Doug House, an Air Force veteran who had volunteered for Lane since 1983. House was hired as Lane's Political Director in 1988 after being laid off from a manufacturing job.

"The Lee campaign was my baby," House remembered. "I was very interested in American History and I viewed working with Lane as being part of that history. We were changing the country."

House's campaign strategy was based on the tried and true tactics of previous election cycles, and then updated to match the current political climate and advances in technology. They also employed several low-budget campaign tactics made famous by Murray Fishel, the one-time director of Political Science at Kent State University. One tactic was positively-reinforced messaging. For example, first Lane's campaign sent questionnaires to their base voters with questions like: "What qualities do you want to see in a candidate?" Answers might include "honesty" or "experienced crime fighter." Then, they'd use those exact terms in mailers and send them back to the base voters. "We'd check for patterns and then repeat the exact phrases from their responses. This type of positive reinforcement was important," House said.

They parlayed this positive reinforcement to their big-budget media buys as well, repeating those popular phrases in their TV and radio commercials. But instead of the typical carpet-bomb approach, they pinpointed specific demographics and mediums. "We targeted farmers with radio ads about the large foreclosure rates and the growing agribusinesses that were buying them out," House recalled. And in the blue-collar metro areas, "We used TV ads for broader concepts, such as the overall failing economic policies of the President (Bush) and how they were hurting workers in Lane's district."

Lane's campaign ads primarily focused on the President and the national Republican platform in general. They tried to avoid referencing Dan Lee by name, so as not to improve his status or name recognition.

"Lane was never addressing or interacting with the opponents," said House. "We didn't want to lend any credibility to opponents. We didn't want to make them congressional, so to speak, or to elevate them."

Dan Lee, to his credit, pushed for a clean campaign. "I tried to run a campaign of ideas, rather than attacking," recalled Lee. "It ran counter to the advice we got from Washington. Namely that if you are a challenger you should attack, attack, attack. We gambled by going in the opposite direction."

And yet, several outside PACs pumped money into local advertising and mailers, each bending the truth and pushing the limits of decency. Lane spoke out against how the national political climate had become noxious. "Never before have I witnessed such a negative campaign season as this one," he wrote in 1990 to the *Dispatch/ Argus*. "Apparently, political consultants are advising their clients that such negative campaigns work. Unfortunately, many candidates are following their advice... With all the problems Congress has with its poor public perception, its credibility won't be restored if it is comprised of 435 mudslingers. So, I ask the voters to examine the candidates with a skeptical eye. Don't rely on thirty-second negative ads to make your important election choices."

"I wanted to believe you could respectfully disagree on the issues, but the political scene was already changing," Lee recalled. "I was at an event and (Republican political strategist) Lee Atwater said that challengers who don't attack are called losers. I wanted to think that he was wrong, that one could appeal to voters based on the issues, but if you look at the election I was in and subsequent developments, the Atwater and Karl Rove brand of politics carries the day. My brand of Republican has by and large disappeared."

Lane won the election on November 6, 1990 with 102,062 votes to Lee's 51,380. It would be the largest margin of victory of any of Lane's elections at 67% to 33%.

Lee blamed the loss on his lack of money as well as President Bush breaking his "Read My Lips, No New Taxes" pledge. But nationally, Democrats only gained one seat in Congress. Doug House credited Lane's massive win more to his constituent services than Bush's broken promise. That year alone Lane's staff had handled over 5,400 constituent cases. "He was always checking to see that cases had been opened on behalf of ordinary citizens regardless of their party or social status," House said. "Everyone in the district either knew him or had met him."

And it was true. Lane was a local celebrity and was at the height of his popularity. He was a geek for technology and knew how to use it to his advantage. Along with his cable-access show, he was also capitalizing on advancements in satellite television transmission that allowed local news stations to transmit live broadcasts from Washington, D.C. Lane held news conferences any chance he got and was always in contact with reporters back home.

He was capitalizing on a technological revolution that transformed politics across the nation. Previously, politicians had been able to have more control over local messaging and media coverage. Few reporters from their home districts would come to D.C., because if they did, they would have to make a tape and then literally send it back to the news station. This meant politicians could take their message back to their district, giving them time to fine-tune their message and deliver their own handpicked information. The satellite transmission gave reporters in Washington the ability to get immediate responses and hold politicians more accountable.

In July of 1987 the *Congressional Quarterly* did an article about this new satellite technology and how young congressmembers who were "raised on television" used the medium to their political advantage. It was called "Hometown Celebrities: the TV Generation in the House," and it featured Lane on the cover. To which Senator Paul Simon commented: "I've been in Washington thirteen years and I've never made the cover of *Congressional Quarterly*. I think that is an indication of the kind of impression that he has made in the Washington scene."

The satellite transmission was equivalent to the "carrier pigeon vs. the wireless telegraph," as the article said: "The ability to dominate the news agenda back home has always been an important protective tool for House incumbents. Now, for those with a high profile on local television, the protective effect is amplified. (Lane) Evans is one member whose security clearly has been bolstered by his status as a local TV star...During his appearances in the district, many greet him with the sort of enthusiasm and adulation that a popular entertainer might receive. Evans' ability to obtain television coverage of his activities helps him offset Republican charges that he is an extreme liberal."

At this time, the media was bound by equal-time laws that mandated that news outlets provide equal time to legally declared political candidates during prime-time, but they were now released from the Fairness Doctrine that mandated news outlets provide "balanced and fair coverage of controversial issues." The Fairness Doctrine was eliminated by Reagan in 1987. Still, many Republicans felt that the local news was unfairly giving Lane too much air time.

To that, News Director Greg Wilson at the Rock Island TV station WHBF (a station known for being conservative) said: "We don't put him on just for the sake of having him on." They only covered him if a local issue was being discussed. And Lane knew that he could spin nearly everything to be local, so he was able to dominate most news cycles even with the most miniscule of issues.

Other House members that were considerably older were upset that they were not getting the same amount of coverage. Lane felt that this was due to a generational difference: "Among some older colleagues, there is some reluctance to use television to get their opinions across." Lane said he was more comfortable appearing on TV because he had been raised on it.

Senior House members like Rep. Pat Roberts (R-KS) lamented the new media focus. Roberts said he was embarrassed by the way his colleagues lined up as if in a cattle chute to give brief comments to TV reporters.

Essentially it was the birth of the sound-bite. A dumbed down, easily digestible snippet of information. And Lane embraced it. He felt it was a quick way to convey information, but in many ways it backfired just as one of the most supported wars in U.S. history was about to take place...

In August of 1990 Iraqi dictator Saddam Hussein ordered the invasion of neighboring Kuwait. At the time, Iraq had the fourth largest army in the world. A coalition of thirty-five countries led by the United States bolstered defense in neighboring Saudi Arabia. That coalition was mostly lip service however, as the U.S. provided over 75 percent of the troops in the region. The effort was dubbed "Operation Desert Shield."

That Thanksgiving, Lane traveled to Saudi Arabia to visit the troops. He ate dinner with them, listened to their concerns, and even participated in morning exercises. Though he had originally supported their deployment, it had become clear that the Bush Administration was pivoting from a defensive stance to an offensive one, so Lane began speaking out against the conflict. Right before Christmas he and forty-five other Democrats filed a federal lawsuit to block Bush from attacking Iraq without the approval of Congress.

Lane wrote Letters to the Editor and lobbied colleagues and held news conferences as often as possible. In January of 1991 he held a Congressional Forum called "Are We Ready to Wage War?" which included retired generals, battlefield doctors, disabled vets, decorated war heroes and experts on battlefield logistics. To open the forum, he said: "The most urgent and immediate questions in the minds of most Americans are the human costs of war. In recent days, nagging questions have surfaced concerning the casualties our young men and women could suffer on the battlefield and the availability of proper medical equipment and supplies. The questions that must be answered are clear—Are our national interests vital enough to justify risking the lives and welfare of American soldiers?"

The forum failed. A few days later, on January 12, 1991, Congress gave the Bush Administration approval to wage war. Over four hundred thousand U.S. troops were mobilized and attacked Iraqi forces on January 17. The conflict was relabeled "Operation Desert Storm."

Lane was not defeated; he knew he still had to fight for the troops. As he later said at a news conference, "We had a long debate in this country about whether we should go to war. But there is no debate about the necessity to support the troops, and that's why, divided as we might have been, we've come together today."

The American people watched their first live war on television. Satellite technology that had transformed American politics now brought the war to our living rooms. Millions tuned in to watch CNN show the aerial attack on Baghdad. Eerie green night vision cameras flashed the glow of bombing raids and artillery tracers.

Within days, stores were filled with patriotic merchandise. Yellow ribbons printed with "Support our Troops" were wrapped around trees, flying from car antennae and pinned to lapels. There were trading cards, board games, and plastic bobbleheads of Chairman of the Joint Chiefs of Staff Colin Powell and Commander of U.S. Central Command Norman Schwarzkopf. It felt more like a sporting event than a war.

And it was over in less than five weeks. After a month-long barrage of air assaults, the U.S. sent in ground forces on February 24th and Iraqi troops surrendered in droves, many hungry and wanting asylum. Bush declared a ceasefire on February 28th.

Saddam's remaining troops then set fire to hundreds of Kuwaiti oil fields and retreated to Baghdad. President Bush decided not to send ground forces into the Iraqi capital to topple Saddam. Instead, the U.S. bolstered defenses in the region and worked to extinguish the fires (the last of which was not extinguished until November 1991). Before the war ended (or at least paused until the 2003 Iraq War), Lane had introduced the Veterans' Compensation Amendment, which would have increased disability compensation and benefits. He also introduced a bill to establish nursing homes and halfway houses that would help veterans readapt to society. Neither made it past committee!

However, the capstone legislation of Lane's entire career became law during the Gulf War: The Agent Orange Act of 1991.

Agent Orange was an herbicide-mixture produced by Monsanto and used as a defoliant during the Vietnam War. Millions of tons were sprayed over crops and thick jungle-cover to expose the North Vietnamese. Roughly two hundred thousand U.S. soldiers were exposed to the defoliant, and many of them became ill upon returning home.

Veterans' groups pressured the government to study the link between Agent Orange exposure and veterans' illnesses, such as rashes, liver dysfunction, infertility, birth defects, and several forms of cancer. Many of the illnesses were invisible, while some Marines broke out in a severe form of acne called chloracne.

From the moment he took office, Lane made Agent Orange a top priority and began working on legislation to compensate and provide care to his fellow veterans. He met a lot of opposition though, even from members of his own party, primarily from the Chairman of the House Veterans' Affairs Committee, Sonny Montgomery (D-MS).

"Sonny thought World War I and II were the real wars, but not Vietnam," Phil said. "He and the VA felt that Agent Orange was just severe acne. We fought them for eight years."

In the early 1980s the Centers for Disease Control (CDC) and the VA started and stopped several studies on the impact of Agent Orange. The most notable was the CDC's Agent Orange Study, a seventy-million-dollar endeavor which began in 1983. It was abandoned in September of 1987 due to what The New York Times called "bitter bureaucratic disagreements over responsibilities and procedures within government." Essentially, the CDC said it was too difficult to locate enough Marines and determine their individual level of exposure.

Lane was livid. And it would only get worse. That same month, a mortality study conducted by the VA was finally presented to Congress, but not until it had already been leaked to the media. As reported by the *Dispatch/Argus*: "The VA completed its study in March but did not report the findings to Congress until September. The VA said they wanted to publish it in a professional medical journal first. Mr. Evans called this incredible."

The VA study showed that Marines in Vietnam had nearly double the rate of non-Hodgkin's lymphoma and a 60 percent higher rate of lung cancer than soldiers who did not serve. It also noted instances of testicular cancer and prostate cancer.

Clearly there was some sort of connection. But at that time, the burden of proof was still on the veteran to prove a link to receive benefits. So, in October of 1987, Lane introduced a bill that would have switched the burden of proof. As Lane told the Southern Illinoisan: "Veterans generally have the legal presumption on their side, that their disabilities are worth something, and the government has to prove otherwise to deny the benefits. In the case of Agent Orange, the reverse is true. Proving the link is, of course, incredibly difficult for your average claimant."

The bill failed to leave committee. Stalled again by Sonny Montgomery.

Undeterred, Lane continued to collect evidence. This included third-party studies by the agricultural and forestry industries that found a link between dioxin exposure and cancer. Also, a 1989 American Legion study that compared troop deployment records with veterans' cancer cases found a higher rate among those who served in defoliated areas.

Lane then introduced his most sweeping bill to date. HR 3004: Veterans Agent Orange Exposure and Vietnam Service Benefits Act of 1989. It had 201 cosponsors and would have given veterans all the benefits they needed.

Though introduced in July, it was again stalled and expired in October with the 101st Congress.

Lane persevered. With the help of the American Legion, Vietnam Vets of America, and the National Veterans Legal Services Program, he presented a comprehensive study to the Agent Orange Scientific Task Force. It was conducted by a team of seven scientists specializing in Agent Orange and led by Dr. Samuel Epstein of the University of Illinois. The study confirmed the results of the VA study, and showed Agent Orange caused other illnesses, including leukemia, pancreatic cancer, brain cancer, and neurological impairment. The evidence was overwhelming.

So, with the U.S. in the midst of the Gulf War and the country in a heightened sense of patriotism, Congress finally paid attention.

Sonny Montgomery introduced H.R. 556: The Agent Orange Act of 1991.

It passed unanimously in both the House and the Senate. President Bush signed it on February 6th.

Lane was one of 71 cosponsors. Beyond that, however, he received no credit.

It was one of the few times Lane was outwardly bitter. A 1991 news release from Lane read: "The legislation was introduced by Rep. Montgomery, who has previously resisted attempts to award disability benefits for Agent Orange exposure. It is virtually identical to legislation Evans authored and failed to pass last year because of time constraints."

Lane was ultimately happy though, as thousands of veterans would now receive the care and benefits they deserved. But the fight wasn't over. There were still the children. Those with birth defects, like spina bifida.

For Lane to be able to pass legislation to help those children, he knew he'd have to topple his nemesis, Sonny Montgomery. He decided to run for the Chair of the House Veterans' Affairs Committee.

But first, he had to get through the 1992 primary and general election. That spring he handily beat former Mercer County Sheriff Richard Maynard in the Democratic primary 47,351 to 10,545. Then in the general election he took on local businessman Ken Schloemer.

Schloemer chaired the Quad City Civic Center Authority and owned a local restaurant. He raised about eighty thousand dollars, with his main donors being John Deere and the NRA.

Schloemer didn't hire a campaign manager, so his campaign consisted mostly of attacks. The most notable was his criticism of Lane's support of gays and lesbians serving in the military, saying that did not represent "Midwestern values." Lane defended his position in the *Quad-City Times*: "I firmly believe that individuals must be evaluated for service based on their own characteristics of fitness. I do not believe in blanket prohibitions against a group of people. As a result, I support lifting the ban on gays and lesbians in the military."

That position was shared by the Democratic presidential candidate, Bill Clinton.

Lane defeated Schloemer 154,029 to 102,512, and Bill Clinton won the White House. "The dawn brings us the first day of a New America," Lane told the *Dispatch/Argus*. "After twelve years of Republican administration, voodoo economics is dead and tomorrow we can go to work on a new economic agenda—putting people first."

That agenda included establishment of the Congressional Progressive Caucus, which he founded with fellow Representatives Thomas Andrews (D-ME), Peter DeFazio (D-OR), Ron Dellums (D-CA), Maxine Waters (D-CA) and Bernie Sanders (I-VT) (who served as the first Chairman). Lane and his fellow progressives wanted to create a universal healthcare system, enlist major education reform, and – of course – establish compensation for veterans' children suffering from spina bifida and other illnesses.

Lane felt that Sonny Montgomery was a barricade to that agenda. So, he decided to run for the Chair of the Veterans' Affairs Committee.

"Lane ultimately challenged Montgomery for chairman after ten years of battling him," Dennis King said. "He informed Montgomery a few weeks before that he'd run against him. Montgomery was a gentleman as well and said, 'I'm sorry you're doing this, but do what you have to do.' Montgomery appreciated the way he handled it."

It drew a lot of attention in Congress, as it was the first time someone had challenged Sonny, and it was the only challenge for a Democratic chairmanship by a rank-and-file Democrat. "You weren't supposed to do that in the old days," Phil said. "But Lane said he didn't care, he wasn't gonna put up with it, and he was gonna take that committee over."

Sonny had been on the committee for twenty-four years and chaired it for the last twelve. He was also a World War II vet and had the support of groups like the VFW, American Legion, and Disabled American Veterans. Lane, meanwhile, launched a heavy negative campaign. He wrote letters to all his Democratic colleagues, and personally lobbied the freshmen congressmen. Democratic leaders tried to discourage Lane, but he refused.

On December 8, 1992, 258 Democrats voted in a secret session. Sonny won 127 to 123.

"I feel good about it," Lane told the *Dispatch/Argus*. "This vote is a clear message for change."

Some believe that Lane was jockeying for a position in the Clinton cabinet. Specifically, as the Secretary of Veterans Affairs (a position which Sonny had helped establish). Lane never received an offer for that position, however.

After the election, Sonny and Lane were called into a closed-door meeting with a handful of high-ranking Democrats, in which both men were scolded for their behavior toward one another. Phil recalled: "The Speaker of the House, Tom Foley, looked at Sonny and said, 'You are wrong, you are dead wrong. Your attitude toward Vietnam vets is appalling.' He really tore into Sonny. Then he turned his guns on Lane and said, 'I want you to work with the Chairman and not get into this tit-for-tat stuff. We don't have time for it.' Then they shook hands and left."

Afterwards, Phil said the two men grew a respect for one another. Sonny took Lane more seriously, and Lane knew that Sonny would now respect his opinion.

In early 1993 Lane returned to Washington, eager to work with the new Democratic president Bill Clinton, who had campaigned on introducing a new Universal Health Care plan. Lane had previously cosponsored the failed Universal Health Care Act in late 1991, and had high hopes in Bill and First Lady Hillary, who was in charge of drafting the Administration's proposal via the Task Force on National Healthcare Reform. Lane met with Hillary and lobbied his colleagues from both sides of the aisle, while championing the issue across the media. As he wrote in a news release: "Caterpillar pays about 60 percent less in health care costs to cover employees in Canada. U.S. firms are forcing workers to take pay cuts or receive less coverage. If the system isn't corrected, plants will close. It is time to create a health care system that serves every American. Businesses would save $4-billion in payroll costs and become more competitive. More money could be invested in expanding operations and job opportunities. This plan is a starting point for making Healthcare a right for every American."

Though he was supporting the health-care proposal, Lane was simultaneously at odds with Clinton on his support of the North American Free Trade Agreement (NAFTA), an agreement that would eliminate nearly all tariffs and trade restrictions among North American countries – and that Lane had been battling against since 1984. The foundation for the agreement had been established with President Reagan and the Trade and Tariff Act, and then President George H.W. Bush had signed the original NAFTA on December 17, 1992. However, it would not take effect until the legislative bodies from Canada, Mexico, and the United States approved it. This gave incoming President Clinton the ability to renegotiate certain aspects of the agreement and time for populists like Lane to hopefully sway his opinion.

Again, Lane took to the media, writing in an op-ed piece for the *Dispatch/Argus*: "For Americans this agreement is a bad bargain. It means American manufacturing and thousands of good-paying jobs move South...NAFTA's approval will put the American middle class on the endangered species list. We will have a society that has two classes, one made up of a small number of very wealthy Americans and the rest who are very poor."

Lane took a lot of heat in return from the local newspapers for his anti-NAFTA stance, primarily because it would help the agricultural sector. Both the *Quad-City Times* and *Dispatch/Argus* took Lane to task for his opposition.

The NAFTA bill was inevitable. The House passed the NAFTA Implementation Act on November 17, 1993 with a vote of 234-200. Lane voted no. But he was not entirely defeated. Clinton ended up adding two amendments to the legislation, the North American Agreement on Labor Cooperation (NAALC) and the North American Agreement on Environmental Cooperation (NAAEC), which included modest protections for workers and the environment. The Senate then passed the act and on December 8, 1993, Clinton signed it into law.

NAFTA was a bitter defeat for Lane. He felt betrayed by his colleagues and his new president. Just a few months later he took another hit, as it became clear the Universal Health Care proposal would never make it to a vote. His high hopes for the Clinton Administration had withered.

During this time, Lane was also searching for answers regarding POWs and MIAs from the Vietnam War. He joined a convoy of veterans and politicians including Senators John McCain (R-AZ) and

John Glenn (D-OH) to Vietnam in the spring of 1993. The purpose of the trip was to uncover the truth about missing U.S. servicemen and review the results of the U.S. Joint Task Force-Full Accounting (JTF-FA), which had conducted a two-year investigation on MIAs and POWs. As he told the *Quad-City Times*: "We're going to convey to the Vietnamese in the strongest terms possible that we must get full and complete answers to our questions."

An April 1993 report from Harvard University had exposed a document from Soviet Communist Party archives which showed the North Vietnamese had held 1,200 POWs in 1972 but officially reported just 368. The JTF-FA had investigated sixty live-sightings of Americans still in Vietnam, along with excavating crash sites and interviewing Vietnamese officials. Ultimately, the JTF-FA found no evidence of any living servicemen.

Though he was coming off three major losses with health care, Vietnam, and NAFTA, Lane was not deterred. "The work goes on, the cause endures," he would say, a line he would often borrow from Ted Kennedy. There were still battles to be had. The children with spina bifida. The thousands of Iraq War veterans. They would all need a champion.

So with record popularity back home and a Democrat in the Oval Office, Lane remained optimistic. He was ready for anything, he said. And in the prime of his life.

Chapter Fifteen

I'm Only Sleeping

August 2010: For Lane's fifty-ninth birthday, his friends gathered at the Renwick Mansion in Davenport, Iowa, a stone Italian-style villa that was built in the 1800s and featured a three-story bell tower with a distant view of the Mississippi River. Depression-era cars lined the long driveway, along with a series of classic Lane Evans campaign signs. The owner was Iowa State Senator Joe Seng and he greeted visitors at the entrance, holding open the massive fourteen-foot wooden doors.

Inside I expected to see a ballroom filled with pearl-clad flappers and gentlemen in top hats, but there was just a handful of people in proletariat attire. The best-dressed visitors were the five sentries there to protect U.S. Senator Dick Durbin. He was a longtime friend of Lane's and had been elected the same year in 1982. Durbin had shed his sport coat and tie to fit in with the rest of the blue-collar crowd.

Cher Erickson was there along with a couple other caretakers and a few former constituent-service employees. Phil Hare and his family attended. As did Galesburg Mayor Sal Garza and a couple other dignitaries. Lane's girlfriend, Erin, was in town and seated next to him at one of the several round tables in the dining room. Lane's hair was disheveled and the top button of his shirt was undone as if he and Erin had just rendezvoused in the closet. Trips like this, even on one of his "good days," were becoming harder to endure.

Everyone ate deli meat sandwiches and generic-brand chips. The Beatles played over a small jambox. We mingled quietly until it was time for the cake. Cher lit the candles and Joe Seng led a rendition of Happy Birthday with his accordion (which was far less tortuous than you'd imagine). Several friends helped Lane blow out the candles.

After cake, Phil gave a speech, as did Senator Durbin. A letter from U.S. Senator Tom Harkin was read aloud, along with a birthday card from President Obama. Obama and Lane shared the same birthday, ten years apart (August 4, 1951 and 1961).

Back in 2004, Obama and Lane had a dual birthday party at the home of Jeremiah Posedel and Anita Decker. Both had worked on campaigns for Lane, and at this time Posedel was the downstate director for the Obama Senate campaign. Decker would later work for Obama at the White House.

That 2004 party was held in their backyard in Moline, just a few days after Obama's star-making-speech at the Democratic National Convention. The twenty-five-dollar per head cookout was officially a campaign fundraiser for Lane, though Obama was clearly the main attraction.

Over three hundred Democrats were scattered about the yard, triple the amount that had seen Obama first speak at the Brew & View. Obama and his wife, Michelle, worked the crowd, posing for pictures and smiling courteously to those who had imbibed a little too much.

After a BBQ dinner, several local politicos gathered on the deck and warmed up the crowd with short speeches and well-wishes. Durbin then took the stage and offered his congratulations to Lane and introduced Obama, who spoke very briefly and thanked Lane for his vital Senate endorsement.

At dusk we all sang Happy Birthday and the two men blew out the candles in unison. Lane opened a few cards with the help of his assistant, Mike Halpin. Obama then got in his RV and continued his tour across Illinois, as Lane was ushered inside to rest on the couch.

It was a unique party, and an unspoken passing of the torch. One man easing into an inevitable retirement, and the other just beginning his rise to power.

Each year, Lane's parties got smaller and smaller. His core group of friends and allies always attended, but even they started dropping off one by one. They'd smile and laugh with Lane, then walk away with a melancholy look on their face. Like they were saying their final farewell.

The parties made him happy, though. They gave him a mental boost for a few days, even if it did sap most of his energy.

A few days after his most recent party in 2010, Lane was visited by Senator Harkin. Erin was still in town and had arranged the visit. Lane was again back in prime form. His mind and body already showing signs of recovery, he was alert and I could even hold a conversation with him. The nutrition and interaction were again working their magic.

For the meeting, Erin dressed Lane in a crisply ironed shirt and combed his hair. Lane even insisted on greeting the Senator in the lobby rather than wait on the couch. Harkin arrived with two body-guards, who stayed downstairs as we all went back to Lane's apartment. Harkin, Lane, and Erin all sat on the couch. I turned off the air-conditioner in the wall to help them hear Lane and we all immediately started sweating. Erin translated for Lane as I sat in the corner and observed, trying not to interject as they discussed the Tea Party movement and Senators selling their seats to the highest bidder.

Harkin and Lane had on the exact same shoes. Black leather loafers with a fake gold buckle. I asked Harkin if they handed those out for free on Capitol Hill. He didn't laugh. I tucked my tail and went to the fridge to get Lane some leftover birthday cake and milk.

The meeting soon evolved into a conversation just between Erin and Harkin. Lane refused to eat the cake, probably because he didn't want to be fed in front of his colleague.

Harkin had a plane to catch. I turned back on the AC and Erin escorted Harkin downstairs.

I stayed with Lane and fed him the cake. It was gone in five bites.

October 28, 2010: I stopped in for a quick visit. Cher's car was in the lot next to Malmstrom's motorcycle. It was strange for them to both be there, so I called before entering the apartment.

"It's not a good day," Cher said. "His blood pressure is low but you can come see if you want." It was 66 over 40.

I hurried upstairs. Cher and Malmstrom were sitting beside him on the couch. His eyes were closed and he was gasping every ten to twenty seconds. Cher had hit the Park Vista emergency button, but they were still waiting for help, so they called 911. Minutes later two medics crashed through the front door. They took his blood pressure, asked about his history, and wrote notes on their latex gloves with a black marker. Lane looked dead the entire time.

Soon they wrenched him off the couch and into a hydraulic gurney. The Park Vista nurse finally showed up. She didn't say a word as we pushed past her to the ambulance.

The cold wind opened Lane's eyes. He looked around bewildered, a baby fresh from the womb. Swirling lights and strange faces. We locked eyes. I'll never forget the fear. The helplessness. The total and absolute confusion. I don't know if he recognized me, but we locked eyes as they pushed him into the ambulance and shut the doors.

I felt like it was the last time I'd ever see him alive.

Cher and Malmstrom followed him to the hospital. I picked up my kids from school and waited for their call.

My phone never rang. I figured no news was good news. But the waiting was unbearable.

November 3, 2010: Cher finally called and said they had X-rayed his lungs for pneumonia and did a bevy of other tests. All came back negative. Cher said that they didn't really know what it was. One of the mysterious perils of Parkinson's. Sometimes the heart just slows down. I wondered how much of it was heartache since Erin had left. Or maybe it was the result of the 2010 elections. Phil had been defeated by Bobby Schilling, an Alleman grad who married into money, sired ten kids, and opened a pizza joint. He ran on the Tea Party platform and was the first Republican to win the congressional seat since Tom Railsback.

I went to see Lane the day after the election.

"We didn't get it done," he said. As always, he said, *We*.

"Phil looked kind of relieved on TV," I offered up the lie. "Almost like he didn't want to win."

Lane didn't reply.

"Who do you think might run next?"

He paused. "Do we have any cookies?"

I smiled. "Probably. I'll check the cupboard."

I brought him a plate of chocolate chip cookies and milk with a straw.

We shared them in silence. Watching the election results on TV. A red sweep of the nation. I think he saw it as his own defeat as well. A rejection of progressivism. Mislabeled populism. That perhaps all his years of work meant nothing. A triumph of the right-wing outrage machine hell-bent on destroying a black centrist president who represented hope and change.

Or, maybe Lane was just sad for his old friend, Phil.

"Have you seen enough?" I asked. He nodded and I turned it to some movie.

He started to doze off. I wiped the crumbs from his chest and I told him I'd see him tomorrow.

But it was a lot longer than that. I needed a mental and emotional break. Maybe we both did.

Chapter Sixteen

We Can Work It Out

Lane had a love-hate relationship with the farmers in his district. Not to mention the businessmen and war hawks. His socially liberal viewpoints turned off many centrists and he was often painted as anti-agriculture by the Farm Bureau and anti-business by the U.S. Chamber of Commerce. Both groups regularly supported his Republican challengers.

Farmers had never forgiven him for resigning from the House Committee on Agriculture after his first term. And they were especially upset at Lane for his opposition to NAFTA (which was a windfall for U.S. agriculture). The fact was, Lane was not anti-farm, he was anti-mega-farm. He had voted in favor of every agricultural appropriations bill since he took office, but opposed measures that he felt benefited the corporate agribusiness rather than the small family farms. When NAFTA was proposed, Lane had conversely supported two alternative initiatives that would have given smaller farms fair and easier access to the global market, the Export Enhancement Program and the Open-Markets and Fair-Trade Act. Both of which failed.

Lane had also sponsored HR 335, a bill that would have allowed farmers to deduct one hundred percent of their healthcare costs; and HR 844, which would have allowed small farm profits to go into an IRA and be exempted from gross income tax. These also failed, but he did have a major success with his support of ethanol subsidies, which benefited corn farmers across the Midwest.

As for the Chamber of Commerce, it was upset with Lane's diehard support of the unions and what they saw as an anti-business agenda. Again, Lane wasn't anti-business, he was anti-mega-business. Lane tried to work hard for the small guys. The entrepreneurs. The innovators. And the old-fashioned mom-and-pop shops that were disappearing due to the ever-increasing power of the corporatists in both parties. The Democratic corporatists were passing new regulations that stifled start-ups, while the Republican corporatists removed regulations that affected labor and the environment. Lane had few friends when it came to his philosophy on business.

Lane believed in using regulations to maintain competition. The very essence of capitalism. He foresaw the dangers of allowing concentration of ownership and fought hard against mergers and acquisitions like the Telecommunications Act of 1996. Lane was one of just sixteen Representatives to vote against the Act, which we now see in 2019 has decimated competition and narrowed media ownership to just a handful of conglomerates.

Lane's efforts for small business often went unnoticed, mostly because his measures rarely passed and small business owners saw a regular increase in taxes and regulations, though many times it came from the municipal or state level. Lane failed to impose tariffs on Chinese goods that were undercutting U.S. companies. He also had a failed bill that would have allowed small businesses to join forces to purchase multiemployer health plans. One of his few successes was when he crossed the aisle to cosponsor HR 3448, the Small Business Job Protection Act of 1996 that provided seven billion dollars in tax relief to small businesses.

Lane's most important contribution to the business community was his support of the Rock Island Arsenal, the weapons and munitions facility that was the district's largest employer. Not to mention the hundreds of small, private companies that depended on it.

So, how could liberal Lane balance the needs of the Arsenal with his belief in tempered military aggression? It wasn't easy. It was a personal struggle that resulted in many charges of hypocrisy. And which was sometimes justified. Several former Arsenal bigwigs assert that he was often unresponsive. That their phone calls and letters were often left unanswered.

Lane also voted against wars that would have directly benefited the facility, namely both the invasions of Iraq. These votes were not anti-war however; they were anti-Imperialist. Lane wanted to protect our young men and women from senseless wars. "Lane rejected the notion that he opposed all war," Dennis said. "He just didn't want misbegotten foreign adventures."

Lane felt the military should only be used in times of homeland defense or truly humanitarian causes. Never in the pursuit of resources nor profit.

This meant creating a streamlined military. One that utilized advancements in technology and unmanned weaponry to protect U.S. soldiers and reduce the number of active personnel. He also wanted to close overseas bases in favor of domestic facilities. So, while his votes may have appeared to be against the Arsenal on the surface (he would vote in favor of military budget cuts under George H.W. Bush and later under Clinton), behind the scenes he was working hard to secure increased funding via earmarks and amendments.

In 1990 during major military budget cuts, Lane authored a successful amendment to the final Defense bill. It reversed proposed workforce reductions at the Arsenal, and authorized $26.2 million in funding for new howitzers.

This was a short-lived victory, however, because in 1991 the Department of Defense was conducting a round of Base Realignment and Closures (BRAC). The BRAC Commission would close or consolidate bases and manufacturing installations across the country as part of an overall military reduction that was ordered during the Cold War. BRAC elicited the General Accounting Office (GAO) to audit facilities nationwide and determine areas for consolidation or downsizing. One of their first recommendations was to move 1,250 Army Materiel Command (AMC) jobs from the Rock Island Arsenal to the Redstone Arsenal in Huntsville, Alabama.

Lane and his colleague across the river in Iowa, Representative Jim Leach, immediately challenged the GAO results. "In the rush to close installations," Lane said in a news release, "there has been a failure to carefully examine all of the facts. Can we confidently say, four months after the (first Iraq) war, that this list will not adversely affect our readiness?"

The two Representatives demanded a review of the GAO results with the hopes of buying time so they would somehow reverse the decision. It was an uphill battle, however. Even the notable U.S. Senator Paul Simon didn't fight. As the *Dispatch/Argus* reported: "Paul Simon all but threw in the towel saying it would be 'very, very difficult' to reverse the BRAC findings. 'I don't want to raise any false hopes.'"

But their strategy worked. The commander of AMC announced they would delay the move until the GAO could explore alternatives, like teleconferencing, rather than physically moving the personnel. The closure was planned but not finalized. Essentially, they would review the closure again in the next round of BRAC in 1993.

And in 1993, the Arsenal gained a reprieve. Newly-seated President Clinton recommended that the Rock Island Arsenal retain those 1,250 jobs based on their ability to "provide excellent customer service and a good labor supply." Clinton's Secretary of Defense, Les Aspin, even proposed moving an additional three thousand jobs from Fort Monmouth in New Jersey!

The BRAC commission still had to officially vote though, and the results were mixed. They voted 6-1 to save the 1,250 Arsenal jobs, but 7-0 against transferring in three thousand jobs from New Jersey. The Arsenal did gain 450 new jobs from the Letterkenny Army Depot in Pennsylvania.

"This is without a doubt the happiest news my district has received in the eleven years I've been in Congress," Lane told the *Quad-City Times.*

BRAC would rear its head again several more times in the years leading up to 2005. Each time, Lane and Leach would join forces to save the Arsenal. They were successful, as the base never had major layoffs until 2005, when roughly five hundred people left the Arsenal's Tank-Automotive and Armaments Command. Sometimes the Arsenal even gained jobs, such as the new Accounting Center that opened in 1995 and added 750 positions.

Ironically, many of those that condemned Lane for being anti-war were often the same people who loved him for supporting veterans.

One of Lane's proudest achievements in the early 1990s was securing benefits for Persian Gulf veterans. Over twenty thousand vets were suffering from hair loss, breathing problems, nausea, and various forms of cancer. People called the sickness "Gulf War Syndrome."

Many doctors believed it was due to veterans being exposed to depleted uranium and chemical fires. Others linked it to the anthrax vaccinations and other inoculations the Pentagon mandated to counteract the effects of biological warfare. But there were no clear studies to date.

Lane believed it was due to their service, so in June of 1993 he proposed a bill that would allow Gulf vets to receive care at VA hospitals without having to prove the ailments were a direct result of their service. As Lane told the *Dispatch/Argus*: "We have to start treating vets now and stop telling them, 'We know you're sick but we don't know why.'" He did not want a repeat of Vietnam and Agent Orange.

According to the Defense Department, the illnesses were the result of pollutants rather than chemical warfare or inoculations. Lane felt this was a cover-up. Sonny Montgomery, however, did not. He had proposed his own bill, which would have also covered the costs for veterans, but capped them after three years even if the vet was still sick. Sonny's bill also allowed cases to be denied if the government could prove the ailment was unrelated to the veteran's service. Lane felt this was a blatant loophole that would allow the government to deny benefits, much like preexisting conditions with insurance companies. Lane's bill had specific parameters for awarding benefits and established an outreach program for vets and their families to learn about said benefits.

It was Lane's bill that would ultimately come to the floor for a vote. It passed unanimously in the summer of 1994.

Though Lane was coming off a series of successes, the rest of the country was not happy. Political divisions were increasing and a Republican wave was forecast in the upcoming midterm election. Lane would face a little-known feed store owner from Aledo, Jim Anderson.

Anderson ran a low-budget campaign comprised mostly of direct-mailers, walking door-to-door, and appearances at parades and coffee shops. Anderson raised just twenty-five thousand dollars and ran no television or radio commercials. Even the Republican National Committee and other PACS did not foresee this district being competitive, so they put very little money into the campaign. Anderson, for his part, though, refused the PAC money that was offered.

The 1994 elections were in fact a Republican Revolution. They gained fifty-four seats in the House and eight seats in the Senate. They even gained twelve gubernatorial seats and gained control of twenty state legislatures. Republicans hadn't held a majority in the U.S. House for four decades.

Lane dodged the slaughter. He beat Anderson by ten points, 55% to 45%, or roughly sixteen thousand votes.

Then a couple months after the election, Lane received some of the worst news of his life. His mother, Joyce, died on January 13, 1995. She had been diagnosed with brain cancer eleven months before. Lane was devastated.

She had been the driving force in his life. Both positive and negative. She was a perennial presence even when she wasn't around, and her apron strings stretched all the way to D.C. He loved her deeply, despite her overbearing nature, and admired her even more. Lane would barely speak about her after she died. As one writer from the *Quad-City Times* said after her funeral: "Try talking to Lane Evans about his feelings and he'll shyly turtle-up, almost embarrassed to give an insight, preferring instead to talk about the mission."

To cope, he poured himself into his work.

He started by proposing several legislative bills aimed at curtailing the negative effects of NAFTA as well as his continued support of veterans. He introduced HR 1278, the Corporate Welfare Reduction Act of 1997, which was meant to reduce energy subsidies and close tax loopholes for U.S. companies doing business overseas. Lane also sponsored HR 1876, to direct the president to support the 1995 UN proposal to eliminate the use and sale of anti-personnel landmines. None of these bills made it past committee.

Lane's one major success at this time was securing benefits to roughly three thousand children of Vietnam vets who were suffering from spina bifida. Lane crafted an amendment to a spending bill that extended benefits to these children. But it also didn't get past committee. So, his friend in the U.S. Senate, Tom Daschle (D-SD), introduced a measure based on Lane's bill. It cleared the Senate 62-35 and a few months later President Clinton signed it into law.

It was yet another personal victory for Lane. Yet again it was credited to another legislator.

One group that did acknowledge Lane's work was the American Veterans Group (AMVETS), the country's largest Congressionally-chartered veterans' organization. In 1995 they awarded him the AMVETS Silver Helmet Award, which was a replica WWII GI helmet made of silver and is considered the "Veterans Oscar." It was, and still is, the most prestigious award given by any veterans organization.

Lane wanted to do even more. A Senate seat would allow him to do so. In late 1995, there were rumors circulating that U.S. Senator Paul Simon was going to retire. Two names immediately came to the forefront as a replacement: Lane and fellow U.S. Representative Dick Durbin (D-IL). Durbin had already started building his war chest while Illinois party leaders gathered to discuss their endorsements.

Most felt that Lane was the best bet though, as he'd never been beaten in an election (Durbin had been beaten twice) and he had a stellar record with veterans. Plus, Lane was about seven years younger and was already being mentioned for future spots on a Democratic presidential ticket.

Simon's retirement was made public and the voters began voicing their support for Lane as well. But just as they were ready to anoint Lane, he suddenly removed his name from consideration. He had shown interest in the seat, but then backed out, and his explanation was unsatisfactory.

"I thoroughly enjoy serving as a House member and believe it is important that over the next eighteen months I continue to devote full attention to the critical issues now being debated in Congress," Lane told the *Quad-City Times*. "I could do a better job as a House member making sure that government remains a positive force in solving the problems that Americans face than as a candidate who must concentrate almost exclusively on raising the estimated eleven million dollars needed to wage an effective Senate campaign in Illinois."

That sounded good. But it wasn't the truth.

Lane had a secret.

A few months earlier he was in a Veterans Day parade in Galesburg, riding in the back of a 1966 Red Mustang Convertible driven by a volunteer named Barb Lafollete.

"He loved the parades," Barb said. "We'd go down and be in line at a certain time, but he knew so many people they followed him like the Pied Piper. It was hard to make sure he got in the car."

Lane sat like a beauty queen, high on the back seat, waving at the people and giving thumbs-ups.

But this year something wasn't quite right.

"He went to wave, and there was something wrong with his arm. He couldn't wave," Barb said.

Lane finished the Galesburg parade, and was then rushed to East Moline and Rock Island to appear in those parades as well. And the same thing happened. All he could do was raise his arm and smile.

"I tried to start waving to the crowd and my hand froze," Lane later told the *Dispatch/Argus*. "I felt something was bad that day."

It was his first public hint of Parkinson's. And it made for a good story. But the truth was, Lane had been having trouble for months and had kept it a secret. He'd been having recurrent back spasms that would sideline him for hours. And once while jogging, he noticed that his right arm was dangling. Doctors first ordered back surgery, which failed to alleviate the pain. They thought perhaps the surgery went wrong, so Lane went to the Mayo Clinic. Doctors there confirmed his worst fear, that he, like his father, had Parkinson's.

Lane confided in his brothers and Erin. And then after the parade incident, he knew he had to come clean. So, he shared the truth with his closest confidants, Dennis and Phil.

They kept his diagnosis a secret from his staff, friends and constituents — for nearly two years.

They feared what it would mean politically, especially as they were about to face their most formidable Republican challenger. A charming, good-looking news anchor from Quincy named Mark Baker.

Baker had quit his job as an evening anchorman to campaign full-time. He went from door-to-door in every district, changing his suit three to four times per day and holding as many news conferences as possible.

Baker had good looks and personality, but his platform was thin and flimsy. As the *Quad-City Times* wrote: "While Baker talks about how conservative he is, he shies away from specifics. For example, he calls himself '100 percent pro-life,' but says he has yet to determine whether he would work to outlaw abortion."

Baker focused more on character and personality than anything of substance. It seemed to work. The U.S. Chamber of Commerce gave him over one hundred thousand dollars, and several other Republican PACs followed suit. Eric Nelson, Lane's campaign manager at the time, begged Democratic leaders for money, but they said

Lane didn't need it. It was a presidential year, and they felt Lane would win handily.

They underestimated Baker, however. His shiny, clean-cut campaign was positive on the outside, while his underlings worked their dirty tricks to undermine Lane. They fueled a whisper campaign that Lane was a homosexual.

At this time, there was a national debate ongoing about homosexual rights. Clinton had recently instituted the "Don't Ask, Don't Tell" policy to protect homosexuals in the military, and it had received a lot of backlash from conservative groups.

There had always been public speculation about Lane's sexuality, and Baker's campaign amplified the rumors. They believed if Lane were a painted as a homosexual it could sway a few undecided voters to the Baker camp.

Lifelong Democrats and many in the general public accepted the rumors as fact. (To the date of this book's publication, the rumor persists.) Lane was a perennial bachelor, he kept his girlfriends a secret, and was on the record as supporting a gay city council candidate in Chicago, so it was easy to believe. Lane just didn't care one way or another.

"They said he was gay because he hadn't married," Dennis King recalled. "Stick that up someone's ass. It doesn't make any difference. He was married to his job. Lane knew that the demands on a wife are too much."

Lane's life was fulfilled with his niece Joyce, his family, and his girlfriend. He never felt deprived or as though he was missing something.

"The more they hit him, the more funny he thought it was," Phil Hare said. "He never took this stuff personally. I met a lot of the women he dated and they were absolutely beautiful. He'd rib me and say, 'Not bad for a gay guy, eh?'"

Lane didn't believe in parading around with his girlfriends. He felt it would be using them as a prop to make a political point. And as far as marriage? Dennis said: "Lane really felt, as a Catholic, he had a calling. He believed his calling was to be a public servant. He didn't want to be married unless he could be a top-notch husband."

Eric Nelson said: "People didn't buy into that because they knew Lane for fifteen years. Everyone knew Lane as Lane. He wasn't Congressman Evans. More often than not, they knew who he was."

Lane won the 1996 election 52% to 47%, 120,008 to 109,240. (William J. Herrmann earned 1% of the vote as a Libertarian.) It was Lane's closest election since 1982. President Bill Clinton won another term, holding off Bob Dole and Reform Party candidate Ross Perot.

Lane made his usual rounds to the front gates at the local manufacturing plants to thank his supporters. Baker, meanwhile, never made a congratulatory call to Lane's campaign and refused to return calls to the local newspapers.

"The only one that didn't thank him was Mark Baker," said Jerry Lack. "All the other guys always called and congratulated him. Baker just wasn't a very friendly guy. A lot of other candidates we'd run into would chat and make small talk. Baker would hardly say hello."

Baker's indignance set the tone for the next election in 1998. It would be a rematch between the two men. This time around the campaign was more negative. And Lane's Parkinson's would play a subtle, yet major role...

"In 1996 people didn't really see the Parkinson's, even though it was affecting him physically," Dennis said. "Then in 1998 he was in denial to himself how much it affected him. You could see it in his facial demeanor. He was always looking stern. So people would ask if Lane was mad at them. He'd say 'No' and try to smile."

The public could tell he wasn't the Lane of old. His handwriting became sloppy. He could barely button his own shirts. And he was unable to stand for long periods of time. Constituents were calling the office saying that it didn't look like Lane "cared" anymore. That he didn't show emotions or expressions about anything.

Unable to hide the disease any longer, Lane knew it was time to let the public know. First, he'd have to tell his staff...

It was on a Monday in May of 1998. Dennis King gathered the D.C. staff at Lane's townhouse and organized a conference call with staff in the Quad Cities. Everyone at the D.C. table sat silently, reluctant to start the conversation. Dennis King finally broke the ice and gave Lane the floor. Lane told them he'd been diagnosed with Parkinson's in 1995.

Some were surprised. Suspicions were confirmed. Yet no one said it was time to retire.

"It was very tough for him to say it," said Eric Nelson. "Then it was like, 'OK, now that we know what is wrong, we can adjust things. We can do what is best and make things easier for you.'"

"I had suspected for a year before," said Lane's personal assistant in D.C., Eda Robinson. "I knew he was getting tests, but I'd try to respect his privacy and not ask questions."

"It was really a shock when he announced," said staffer Karri Gelski. "He started losing some weight and what not. He started getting thin. Stiffer and slower, but it wasn't anything completely obvious."

A week before the meeting, Lane had been in a deep depression. After the confession to his staff though, he felt the proverbial weight lift off his shoulders.

"It was one of the best conversations of my life," he told the *Quad-City Times*. "I remember the next day I was out running, and for fifteen to twenty minutes I didn't even think about Parkinson's, when before I was just completely obsessed."

On May 18, 1998, Lane announced his disease to the public. The story was plastered across the local media, but Lane felt little backlash. The public accepted it as a reasonable explanation, or justification, for his changed demeanor. His ability to perform the job was yet to be questioned.

"I live for this job," Lane told the *Dispatch/Argus*. "I live for helping people who don't have any other advocates and I just want to continue doing the job that I've been doing. I do have problems in terms of standing in particular, sometimes having difficulty moving around, and sometimes I think I'm smiling when I'm not. But I feel fine otherwise, and I'm ready to do what it takes in this campaign to take it directly to my opponent."

"He was inspiring 'cause that Marine in him just kicked in," said Robinson. "He was like, 'Well, I'm still Lane, we're still gonna do the job.' I had noticed a bit of the leg shaking and didn't quite know what that was. Once they narrowed it down and got him on his regimen of meds he did pretty good. The police officers at the Capitol were good about looking out for him. He always walked home one to two blocks from the office."

"That's when I learned to admire Lane even more. That even with his disability, he went out in public," said Ginny Shelton. "So many people hide. Lane went out in public. Lane was telling everyone that 'yeah, I have a disability but I can still do my job.'"

Other local and national Parkinson's patients rallied in support, and several called the office to thank him for his bravery. As Ginny said: "One guy in particular said, 'Lane gave me so much courage. Because of my handshake I stopped meeting my friends for breakfast. Now Lane gave me the courage to go meet my friends for breakfast again.'"

The reaction from Baker was curt yet cordial. He immediately released a statement wishing the best for Lane and his family. A day later, Baker questioned his delay in telling the public. To his credit, Baker never directly brought up Parkinson's; however, he did try to imply that Lane was too weak to serve. He challenged Lane to debate in all fourteen counties of the 17th district, perhaps knowing that Lane couldn't meet the schedule.

"Parkinson's was starting to really affect him," Jerry Lack said. "He'd get tired earlier and it affected his communication and speaking ability. It was hard. A young Lane would have defeated Baker in a debate handily."

Eric Nelson deflected in the *Dispatch/Argus*, turning the reason for a lack of debates onto Baker: "We'll make a decision on a debate schedule when Mark Baker makes a decision on what he stands for and what he wants to talk about." Baker was still avoiding specifics and giving ambivalent answers, hoping to ride his telegenic looks into office.

The midterm race drew national attention and was considered a toss-up, as Democrats were fighting to retake control of Congress. Baker had spent the past two years working a cushy job with the U.S. Chamber of Commerce and they, along with John Deere and national conservative PACs, filled his coffers with over one million dollars. Lane too raised over a million dollars, funded mostly by unions, liberal PACs, and national Democrats. It was Lane's most expensive campaign to date. They had spent a combined one million dollars two years before.

Most of that money was spent on television. The candidates tripled their amount of television ads, and unfortunately, most of the ads were negative. Lane did air several positive commercials though. One in particular showed him jogging on the National Mall in Washington D.C. It was meant to undermine any insinuations that Lane was weak or not "up to the job." And the ad wasn't misleading, as Lane still jogged every morning and lifted weights twice per week to keep his muscles limber — an integral part of Parkinson's treatment.

There was one weakness that Baker was successful in exploiting: In October, Lane voted in favor of an inquiry of impeachment against President Clinton. The President had engaged in a now-infamous sexual relationship with intern Monica Lewinsky beginning in 1996. The affair became public in January of 1998, captivating the nation and setting Republicans on a relentless series of investigations meant to prove that Clinton not only had the affair, but lied about it under oath. After months of investigating, Clinton testified before an independent counsel and gave a prime-time national speech admitting to his relationship with Lewinsky.

On October 8, 1998, Lane joined a mere thirty other Democrats to vote in favor of the impeachment inquiry. This was in spite of national polls showing that the majority of the public was not in favor of the investigation. Lane explained his vote in the *Dispatch/Argus*: "I believe the interests of our nation require us to review the issues presented by the Independent Counsel. It is also in the interest of the President that we find facts and resolve questions. I will keep an open mind and carefully examine the evidence and work for a resolution that puts the interests of our nation first."

"He caught a lot of crap on impeachment," said Nelson. "He was voting to have a full investigation because if you don't have a full investigation, you run the risk of people thinking you have a cover-up. A lot of Democrats were pissed off over the vote."

Lane's opponent from 1990, Dan Lee, summarized the issue as a columnist for the *Dispatch/Argus*: "By voting for the GOP proposal, Mr. Evans voted against the preferences of a substantial portion of the Democratic base. That could prove to be costly to Mr. Evans... In an era in which cynicism runs rampant, he deserves a substantial measure of credit for putting principle ahead of expediency."

Lane won the midterm election on November 3, 1998 52 percent to 48 percent, by just 6,056 votes.

"The last one was sweet, but this one was so massive in effort...it was very gratifying," Lane said in a victory press conference.

The morning after the election, Lane made his standard appearance at local factory gates to shake hands with his blue-collar supporters. Meanwhile, the media was unable to reach Baker for comment and he never called to congratulate Lane. Rock Island County Republican chairwoman Bess Meersman told the *Quad-City Times* that Lane was too sick to finish the term. "I feel he will not be in (Congress) the whole two years" and that he was simply "keeping the seat warm for a hand-picked successor."

To that Lane replied: "I'm not going to spend one million dollars of people's money and then work for six months and resign." He also noted that if he did have to quit midterm, there would be a special election and Baker would probably win.

Both sides had spent more than a million dollars and the results from the last election were hardly changed.

"In 1998 a million dollars was spent and like four people changed their vote," Dennis laughed. "We could have spent one hundred thousand dollars in '96 and saved a million in '98. But, the Baker campaigns got Lane reintroduced to the public. He knew tough campaigns were a good thing because it gave the public a new image of him."

And Lane would need that new image. The fighter in the face of Parkinson's. He would continue working on behalf of the people, despite his own illness.

In two years, he would face Baker yet again but in the meantime, he continued his fight for veterans and the downtrodden.

Lane sponsored several bills including the Veterans Chiropractic Care Act, Department of Veterans Affairs Employment Reduction Assistance Act, Veterans' Access to Emergency Care Act, Veterans' Hepatitis C Act, Justice for Atomic Veterans Act, Persian Gulf War Veterans Health Care and Research Act and many more. It wasn't just veterans, however; he co-sponsored the International Child Labor Relief Act, Clean Air Common Sense Act, and the School Construction Act. Like many times before, none of these bills made it past committee.

The few bills he sponsored or cosponsored at this time that did become law included the Torture Victims Relief Act, which authorized the President to provide assistance to foreign victims of torture. He also helped pass the Veterans Programs Enhancement Act of 1998, which granted increases to education, housing and cemetery programs for veterans. Other laws, which were self-explanatory by definition, included the Great Lakes Fish and Wildlife Restoration Act, Church Arson Prevention Act and the Veterans' Compensation Cost-of-Living Adjustment Act. Lane also voted in favor of giving the Congressional Gold Medal to Nelson Mandela.

On March 3, 1999, Lane's father Lee Evans died from complications due to Parkinson's disease, less than a year after Lane had made his own affliction public. Lee had kept the disease relatively secret, aside from a circle of friends, family, and his caretakers in the nursing home. The disease wasn't even mentioned in his obituary.

The family had a private ceremony in Rock Island and from that point on, Lane spoke little of the loss of his father or mother. He would only say that they were great people, who taught him much, and then refuse to answer any other questions. Much of it had to do with his own realizations of mortality. Lee had also suffered from Lewy body dementia, so watching his father lose his awareness and cognizance was not only disheartening, but a painful foreboding of his own future.

In 1999, the U.S. economy was booming. The Internet bubble was inflating (it wouldn't burst until March of 2000) and companies were spending millions preparing for the predicted Y2K catastrophe. President Clinton had survived his impeachment. Jobs were plentiful. And the stock market was setting records.

The country headed into the new century, which would begin with a new Presidential election. Then-Vice President Al Gore would take on George W. Bush, while Lane would face Mark Baker yet again.

This time, Baker brought in the big guns to stump for him. This included House Speaker Dennis Hastert (who would later serve 13 months in prison for bank fraud in an attempt to silence a high-school boy he had sexually abused), vice-presidential candidate Dick Cheney, and Senator John McCain (R-AZ). Lane countered with visits by Al Gore and his running mate Senator Joseph Lieberman (D-CT).

Baker again challenged Lane to several debates, and Lane dodged them. Lane knew that the Parkinson's had affected his speech and motor skills so much that he would lose the debates, even if his arguments were more solid. Appearances mattered, and it would have been hard for the sloth-faced Lane to defeat the charismatic TV personality.

Eric Nelson was still Lane's campaign manager, and the excuse he gave to the media was that Baker's campaign was "engaging in push polling, a disreputable political practice in which a campaign spreads rumors about its candidate."

It was true. There were many rumors swirling through the public, implying that Lane was unable to perform his duties. The Baker campaign never explicitly said that Parkinson's would affect Lane's ability to hold office, so side-groups and PACs did the dirty work for him. They implied it in mailers, commercials, and flyers on windshields.

"The tactics of the Republican party to make Parkinson's an issue is an insult to the entire disabled community," Lane told the Peoria (Illinois) Journal Star. "It's being done by educated people who know better."

Baker was targeting independent and Democrat voters which he felt could be swayed. He told the *Quad-City Times* that he felt there was still a reservoir of undecided voters: "Definitely there are votes being changed," Baker said. "How big a pool that is, it's hard to say, but it's definitely enough to make a difference."

Lane felt differently. At the annual Rock Island County Labor Day picnic, he told a mass of cheering voters that: "there are few minds that aren't already made up about this race. There's no one who will ever defeat me as long as you're in my corner." Lane felt that turnout would be the deciding factor.

On November 7, 2000, Lane beat Baker by the biggest margin of the three contests, 10 points. 55 percent to 45 percent. 132,494 to 108,853. Al Gore also won the 17th District, 53% to 43%.

Gore won the popular vote nationally, but the results of the Electoral College votes wouldn't be known for months. There was an issue of "hanging chads" and ballot recounts in Ohio and Florida. The issue went before the Supreme Court and George W. Bush was declared President in December 2000.

Needless to say, Lane was unhappy, but he would honor the results.

It was another setback in an already miserable year. His father had died, the Parkinson's was beginning to take a heavier toll on his body, and his lifelong companion Erin had received a job offer from California Governor Gray Davis.

Lane told her, "Go for your dreams, Babe. This is the time. It's good for us to take this break." He said that he didn't want the disease to bring them both down. Years earlier, they had discussed marriage but they both understood that their relationship was secondary to their careers. With a heavy heart, Erin moved to the opposite coast.

At the same time, Lane's beloved niece Joyce was going off to college and Doyle had plans to move within the year. To top it all off the initial effects of Lewy body dementia were beginning to manifest.

"We were worried because he was on the medications and he was getting worse. He started to just renovate his house for no reason. Just to spend money," Deirdre said. "He was becoming unable to be independent, so maybe since he couldn't control what was happening to him physically, he tried to control his home environment."

Lane spent frivolously for the first time, purchasing Roman columns for his townhouse and other materialistic garbage he would have never considered in the past. He would also go to big galas and events that he'd previously shunned, flirting with women he would never have shown interest in before. It was like a midlife crisis. Perhaps he was realizing he only had a few years left of mobility and mindfulness.

Things would only get worse. The 2000s would be tumultuous: 9/11. War. Elections. Retirement. The upcoming years would be the most challenging of Lane Evans' life.

Chapter Seventeen

Don't Pass Me By

December 2010: I hadn't seen Lane in six weeks. And for the first time, I didn't care. I didn't feel bad. Each time I went to see him he was more of a void, a shell of a man. He mumbled worse and I could barely understand what he was saying. All he did was sit in front of that television. Time was arbitrary. A day was a week was a month was a day. I could get away with fleeting visits and act like I'd been there every day.

This is what happened since losing his round-the-clock care. Cher would stop by for short visits, and his physical and medical needs were met, but he seemed lonely.

It was like the solitude had made him crawl into himself. Amplified the dementia. Or maybe he was on new medications. A higher dose perhaps. Whatever it was, he couldn't even answer my questions anymore. Granted, he was never able to answer complex questions like, why did you vote in favor of decreasing the top marginal tax rate in 1986? Or, why did you vote against hydropower on the Mississippi? But now even the simplest questions were over his head.

"Who were some of your best friends in the Marines?"

He looked at me confounded, then mumbled something like, "I don't remember."

"Did you ever wish you went to Vietnam instead of your brother?"

"I'm slipping. I'm slipping," he replied.

I got up and left. I felt nothing. Like so many others, I'd become indifferent.

He was no longer the man I knew.

I went to see him on December 23rd. No Christmas gift in-hand. No card. Not even a bag of candy. I knew what I'd be walking into.

And there he was. On the couch. Ice Age 2 blaring from the television. He looked up at me. No smile, no recognition. Just an empty stare. Exactly what I expected.

"Hey Lane, how are you doing?"

No answer.

We sat in silence for a bit.

"Can I have that water?" he rasped.

I pointed at the glass already on the tray in front of him. He began to drink from the straw and a nurse walked in with his lunch. It wasn't the hulk-nurse but she seemed just as tough. A brunette with an Eastern European accent. She pulled him to his feet and pushed him into the bathroom. I listened: "Pants off. Sit. Shit. Wipe. Ok, get up. No, no don't sit. Your friend is waiting for you. Stand up."

I thought about running, half-afraid that she might come for me next. Lane would never know the difference. I had last-minute shopping to finish. Presents to wrap.

But I waited. She got him back to the couch and brought his lunch. I told her I'd feed him, and she left.

"Is there anything special you want the next couple days?" I asked, looking at his pitiful meal. "Some turkey? Or sausage pizza?"

He didn't answer. I knew what he wanted. Respite. Release. Rejuvenation. Reunions with lost loved ones. Things that I couldn't give.

I wished Erin were back. Feeding him greens and fruits and nutritious concoctions from the blender. Holding him. Talking to him. Walking him up and down the halls. He was lucid then. Clear-minded.

He needed that constant companionship, but I had my own family and commitments, and so did Cher and Malmstrom. We only had so much time to share. And right now, I was tired. I didn't have it in me anymore.

It was a feeling I'm sure many friends and caretakers of Parkinson's patients feel. It takes a toll. Sometimes you almost just wish the end would come. For their own sake as well as your own callous self-protection.

In some ways Lane's dementia was a gift. He wasn't witnessing the passage of time or fretting about his impending death. Contemplating mortality or questioning the after-life. Dementia, like senility, could be nature's way of helping people deal with their inevitable fate. Lane it seemed, was blessed with oblivion.

I tried to feed him the lunch, but he didn't want anything. It was the first time I'd seen him refuse a meal. So, I set the fork down and waited. We watched the end of the movie. Soon he dozed off.

"Ok, well I'll see you Lane. Happy Christmas."

I grabbed my coat and walked out. Unsure of when I'd return.

June 13, 2011: Six months passed and I visited sporadically. My wife was being transferred to Omaha for work so our family was preparing to move. I went to tell Lane the news.

I knocked and went in. The TV was off. Cher was there. Laughing and smiling with Lane on the couch. He had clean clothes and looked freshly showered.

"What's up?" I asked, completely surprised by the scene before me. It was like I'd gone back in time.

Lane was awake and cracking jokes! He was aware, annunciating, and acting a decade younger. It was a complete reversal. Cher was beaming too.

Was he on a new drug? Did they find a cure? I wondered.

Cher told me that Obama was coming to town and wanted to have a private meeting with Lane.

Lane smiled then. An actual smile that came from someplace deep within. It was like he was important again.

Cher asked if I'd like to tag along.

"Of course," I told her.

Seeing Lane so excited slightly overshadowed my guilt for deserting him for the past few months. It was still no excuse for my abandonment. I had given up on him, like so many others, when all he needed was a purpose. A goal to work towards. It had given him new life.

June 28, 2011: After two weeks and a few interviews with the Secret Service, we were cleared for the private clutch with the President. Not at the White House; Obama was visiting the Alcoa plant in Davenport, Iowa.

I rendezvoused with Cher and Lane in the Alcoa parking lot, and got Lane's wheelchair out of the trunk. He was dressed in a blue plaid shirt with a tan tie. Cher wore a summer blue dress. I wore a fancy tan suit but felt ridiculous, because I had shaved my head for the first time as a tribute to one of my best friends who had recently died.

We went through three security stations and were taken to a small office.

I started an audio recording on my flip-phone and set it on a small bookshelf:

(President Obama walks in, and gives Lane a hug.)
Obama: *Lane! How you doing!*
Lane: *Good.*
Obama: *Good to see you buddy, how you been. Long time no see.*
(Turns to me, shakes hand.)
Me: *Hello Mr. President.*

Obama: *Hey Devin how you been?*
Me: *Good, good.*
(I take my seat next to Lane.)
Obama: *Lane, how you been doing? You doing ok? Doing all right?* (Looks to Cher) *She takin' good care of you, I know she is.*
(Lane laughs.)
Obama: *So, it's great to see you.*
(Turns to Secret Service and others behind him.)
Obama: *My earliest supporter downstate, I would never be president if it hadn't been for this man...cause I wouldn't have won the Illinois Senate without this guy.*
(Hurumphs.)
Obama: *You know, Alcoa's doing good here.*
(The President is resorting to small talk? Was he nervous? Upset at seeing his old mentor so haggard?)
Obama to Cher: *So, what else has been going on around here?*
Cher: *Just getting through the day.*
Obama: *Yeah, yeah.*
(Turns to me)
Obama: *Devin, how you been man? Whatch you been up to?*
Devin: *Actually, I'm writing a bio on Lane.*
Obama: *Oh, that sounds fun. So, the uh, so the uh. So, you gotta get that book out man. That will be exciting.*
Cher: *Should be done by the end of the summer, right?*
Me: *Hopefully.*
(Obama stands)
Obama: *Ok, so let's get a good picture going. I'm gonna stand right behind Lane.*
(Pictures are taken. I hand him a pic to sign for my daughters. As he's signing it, Lane motions to me and says something about support, so I chime in.)
Me: *Lane wants to say that he's really supporting you.*
(What the hell does that mean? It was a horrible, tongue-tied attempt at a compliment.)
Obama: *Well, look. Lane, you've always been the greatest of friends, so if there's anything that we can do, you just need to let me know. All right. You guys have Reggie's email? Hey Reggie!*
(Reggie Love, Obama's assistant, comes in)
Obama: *So, Reggie's always with me Lane, so if you guys need any-thing, all you gotta do is just send Reggie an email. Anything that we can be helpful to you let us know.*
(Reggie Love turns to me, and we shake hands.)
Obama: *And I want a copy of that book when it gets written. All right?*
(President Obama pulls me in for a "bro hug.")

Obama: *All right. Thanks Man. It's great to see you.*
(President Obama kisses Cher on the cheek.)
Obama: *Good to see you Man*
(He hugs Lane.)
Obama: *All right. Thanks a lot.*

June 30, 2011: Two days later, I went to see Lane and brought a few photos from our meeting with Obama.

I knocked. No one answered. I went inside.

The entire apartment was a mess. There was literally a smear of shit across the kitchen floor. Lane was standing in the living room in sweat pants, a stained sweatshirt and, from the smell of it, a heavily-soiled diaper.

My hands shook, and my breathing staggered. A mix of rage and pity.

This was Lane Evans. Just days after meeting with the most powerful man in the free world.

"Is it 10 a.m. or 5 p.m.?" he asked. I gently took him by the arm and walked him to the couch.

"10 a.m."

He broke into a song: "Let it be, Let it be..."

I said something that I don't remember. I didn't know what to think or do.

"Here's what I need to make due," Lane said. "I'll probably need three to four..." he trailed off and his eyelids slowly closed. I perched a pillow under his arm and left. I went to the nurse's station and demanded that they go help him. They hurried upstairs.

Later I called Cher and told her. She said she'd found him that way before too. She'd discuss it with management.

I didn't see him again for months after that, as I was traveling back and forth to Omaha.

That autumn, Cher and Malmstrom worked on finding Lane a new home.

Chapter Eighteen

A Hard Day's Night

It was a new century. A new millennium. And a new president. True, it technically didn't start until 2001, but the country and the world viewed 2000 as a new beginning. We had expected flying cars, world peace, and robotic maids; however, it was ushered in with war, terror, and an economic assault on the lower class.

The 49-year-old Lane Evans was starting his tenth term in Congress and was the ranking Democrat on the House Veterans' Affairs Committee. According to the *Dispatch/Argus*, Lane was "surprisingly cheerful for a liberal Democrat facing another two years of minority status on Capitol Hill and a new Republican president."

Lane's optimism was a facade, however. On top of his physical struggles, he knew what sort of agenda he'd face. The first order of business by popular vote loser George W. Bush was to get Congress to pass a new budget and an enormous $1.6 trillion tax cut, citing the $3.1 trillion projected budget surplus from the Clinton administration as justification. Critics said it would be a dramatic redistribution of wealth from the lower class to the upper class, while proponents trumpeted the benefits of trickle-down economics.

House Minority Leader Dick Gephardt urged his fellow Democrats to work on a bipartisan bill. In a memo Gephardt wrote on February 22, 2001, he said: "Republicans must work with Democrats to craft a bipartisan approach to a budget. Democrats want to debate fully all aspects of budget policy BEFORE passing a tax cut. Then we should debate what kind of tax cut is most fair for all Americans."

The Republicans then presented their budget and it was just as detrimental as Lane expected. Gephardt wrote another memo to his colleagues in March: "The combination of tax cuts and defense spending increases will mean that Social Security and Medicaid trust funds will be invaded to fund other government programs. As Democrats, we can challenge the President's priorities and propose a significantly different budget. But given the President's insistence on his program, there is little likelihood we would influence the outcome. Confrontation would result in partisan debates and battles, but little else."

Lane felt that Gephardt's call for collaboration would set a precedent of weakness. The days of compromise seemed to be ending. And with this President, Lane felt a compromise was capitulation. He wanted to take a more adversarial approach, so he let his colleagues know via letters and phone calls and speeches on the House floor. But his words fell on deaf ears. The Economic Growth and Tax Relief Reconciliation Act passed 240–154 and President Bush signed it into law in June of 2001.

Lane called a news conference a few months later condemning the fact that Bush's budget was already eating into the surplus and that Republicans were readying cuts to Social Security and Medicare. "This is a real, unimaginable turn for the worse," Lane said. "President Bush promised that his tax cut would not come at the expense of our nation's seniors."

The issue was quickly forgotten, however. The dwindling surplus and increase in deficit spending was overshadowed on September 11, 2001.

9/11 was a terrorist attack on the World Trade Center and Pentagon carried out by nineteen hijackers, mostly from Saudi Arabia, and masterminded by Al-Qaeda leader Osama bin Laden. They flew two commercial airplanes into New York's World Trade Center Twin Towers, and a third into the Pentagon. A fourth plane crashed in Shanksville, Pennsylvania, after passengers fought to overtake their hijackers. It was one of the major turning points in American history.

Congress immediately passed sweeping homeland security measures and organized a military response against Al-Qaeda in Afghanistan, which came to be known as Operation Enduring Freedom, presently the longest ground war in American history.

With passage of the USA Patriot Act, the surveillance powers of the government against private citizens were dramatically increased. Fear had captivated the nation. And in the heat of the moment U.S. citizens traded their privacy for security, which some might argue was a victory for bin Laden. He had succeeded in transforming the USA from a free society into a virtual paranoid prison state.

To help combat the anti-Muslim and anti-immigrant fervor, Lane co-sponsored H. Res. 255 with Rep. Mike Honda and other members of the Congressional Human Rights Caucus. The resolution was meant to help curb the growing hate-crimes and violence wrongly targeting the turban-wearing Sikh population. The resolution declared that "in the quest to identify, locate, and bring to justice the perpetrators and sponsors of the September 11, 2001 terrorist attacks on the United States, the civil rights and liberties of all Americans, including Sikh-Americans, should be protected." Unfortunately, the resolution never made it out of the Judiciary Committee.

Meanwhile, Operation Enduring Freedom would mean a boon to defense contractors and US arsenals. Lane lobbied heavily on behalf of the Rock Island Arsenal for an upcoming defense spending bill, accentuating their readiness and production capabilities. In December, Republicans presented and passed a $343 billion defense bill that included fifteen million dollars for the Rock Island Arsenal and spared them from another round of Base Realignment and Closures (BRAC). An easy win for Lane and the Quad Cities.

A year passed and the war in Afghanistan continued. Lane did what he could on a domestic level. Not to mention his personal struggles with life, love, and Parkinson's.

First and foremost was helping to find a cure for Parkinson's, along with managing his own symptoms. There was progress being made in Parkinson's research utilizing stem cells. But in 2001 Bush signed an Executive Order that curtailed federally funded stem-cell research and limited any stem-cell research to just existing colonies of cells.

Lane sent letters to all his colleagues, hoping to overturn the president's decision. He cited progress that was made by the National Institutes of Health in utilizing stem cells from surplus embryos at fertility clinics. He also commented on the possibility of using stem cells from mice, since Bush's main concern was the use of human embryos, but noted that alternative stem-cell pools were unlikely to emerge in the near future.

"We must overturn the president's decision and restore hope to those who struggle every day to survive their afflictions," Lane said in his letter. "This is a serious threat to the science of stem-cell research and future medical advancements in the field." He cited progress that could be made in researching Multiple Sclerosis, Alzheimer's, and spinal cord injuries.

Despite the support of many Democrats, the stem-cell research limits remained (until Obama overturned them in March 2009). Lane and fellow Parkinson's patients were left to rely on existing treatments.

Lane continued to jog every day, along with a routine of stretches and mental exercises. He performed controlled breathing and meditation that he learned from the D.C.-based Center for Mind-Body Medicine, an alternative therapy center that he had been visiting since his first diagnosis. The treatments included biofeedback, drawing, guided imagery, and journaling. (One of his first journal entries was, "I feel like a prisoner.")

Overall, Lane was completely focused on staying fit to serve.

"We talked about alternative therapies such as chiropractic, massage therapy, acupuncture, etc.," recalled one of his staffers, Bev Strayhall, who was also a nurse. "He was so determined to do everything he could to stay in shape physically, mentally, and spiritually. He really seemed hopeful and optimistic that these types of activities could be therapeutic."

The results of these therapies were hard to determine, but he definitely seemed to be managing his symptoms. The disease would always progress, however, as he was starting to have trouble pushing buttons in elevators and turning small knobs on electronics. The long-term effects of his alternative therapies would be nearly impossible to track, but at the time they were undoubtedly beneficial to Lane.

Lane also had simple short-term goals, which was pretty much not to embarrass himself. "I remember him telling me a story about Janet Reno (Attorney General under Clinton who also had Parkinson's) falling off a curb in D.C., and he was trying to stay in shape so that sort of thing didn't happen to him," said Strayhall.

At this time a new woman entered Lane's life, a Korean professor working in the U.S., OkCha Soh. She had first met Lane in 1999 at a fundraising event shortly after Erin had left for California. Lane was on the rebound, so he invited OkCha to a Christmas ball with then-President Clinton. After joining him at such an exclusive event, OkCha was enamored.

The two were together frequently at OkCha's behest, and the local media began to notice. Lane's once shielded personal life was now under scrutiny.

Lane told the *Quad City Times* that she was just a "good friend." But the reporter noted that "the proof that she is his companion stands in his Capitol Hill office. His wall collection of Beatles photos and other memorabilia now includes a framed photo of them posing with former President Bill Clinton and Sen. Hillary Clinton at a recent ball."

The relationship lasted into the next presidency and OkCha urged him to attend the parties and fundraisers that he had once shunned. "He had a lot of official events. Almost every evening I accompany him," OkCha said in her broken English. "We always go together to the White House for annual party. I was wearing a Korean dress and President Bush always admired my Korean dress."

The two also went shopping frequently. "When he buy stuff for himself, he always go for the cheap, humble stuff," OkCha said.

"Whenever he buy for me, he always take me to very expensive place. I say 'stop, stop.' He had a giving heart."

OkCha soon moved into Lane's townhouse, but Lane voluntarily slept on the couch. Some say that OkCha was controlling like his mother, which comforted Lane. He was able to relinquish some control and to focus on his career, while OkCha handled his personal affairs.

Lane suddenly found himself championing issues that were out of his normal realm. Not that they were any less deserving. They were just different. Primarily it was the issue of Korean "comfort women," an issue that OkCha had championed for many years as the president of the Washington Coalition for Comfort Women Issues.

Japan had enslaved thousands of Korean women during the 1930s and 1940s to be used as "comfort women" in brothels for Japanese imperial soldiers. OkCha and other Korean activists worked for years to bring international attention to the issue or get some sort of recompense.

In 2001, Lane introduced a resolution in the House that asked Japan to "formally apologize for its role in forcing women into sexual slavery during the World War II era." Lane told the *Dispatch/Argus*: "It has been almost 56 years since Japan surrendered to the Allied powers. Very few comfort women survived, and time is running out for Japan to properly account for its actions. We must act now and remember that there is no statute of limitations on crimes against humanity."

The resolution did not immediately result in any action by Congress nor Japan. OkCha and Lane were disappointed, but not defeated. He would bring it up again in three years.

In 2002, Lane faced a new contender for his congressional seat, a political newcomer from Galesburg, Pete Calderone. Calderone worked as a self-employed fishing tackle sales representative and had no experience in how to run a campaign. Lane had an obvious advantage with his experience and incumbency, not to mention a freshly gerrymandered district.

The 17th district had just been redrawn based on the 2000 Census and Lane benefited heavily by design. His old friend Bill Lipinski had worked out a compromise map with Speaker Dennis Hastert (R-IL) that they called the "incumbent protection plan."

"We were trying to set up the best map for Lane," recalled Lipinski. "The map Dennis proposed had Lane getting eliminated. I said, 'We can't do that!' I insisted on a good district that he could win. It was one of the most gerrymandered."

"It was a better district, but it wasn't a slam dunk," Dennis King countered. "A lot of Democrats in the 17th are more conservative. A strong Republican can beat someone in the 17th; it was only 53 percent Democrat."

In most political gerrymandering, the maps resemble a Rorschach test. In this case it looked like a seahorse creeping along the Mississippi River then curling into the center of the state.

Of the district, the *Quad City Times* wrote: "The new 17th District now cuts a narrow swath along the Mississippi River, then juts east to lop off a portion of Springfield and most of Decatur, Ill. This oddball district brings in the mix of rural, agricultural and urban manufacturing towns that defined the old 17th. Evans has proven effective at representing that kind of district."

Meanwhile a wave of ~~Patriotism~~ (sic) Nationalism was sweeping the country, fueled by messages from the Bush White House that Iraq was an imminent threat to humanity. The U.S. was still fighting in Afghanistan, and now the Bush White House wanted to preemptively invade Iraq based on sketchy intelligence that dictator Saddam Hussein was stockpiling weapons of mass destruction (WMDs). Secretary of State Colin Powell testified in front of the United Nations that Iraq was hiding WMD, while Secretary of Defense Donald Rumsfeld said there was indisputable evidence that Saddam was planning to launch missiles tipped with biological agents. Through it all, the entire administration claimed that Saddam and bin Laden were partners in war crimes.

There was little evidence to support their claims. Intelligence reports ran contrary to the information coming out of the White House. In a nutshell, and some may argue this, Saddam thought he had WMDs based on falsified information from his underlings, and the White House used that baseless information to justify the war.

National polls showed two-thirds of Americans supported the war. Yard signs proclaimed WE Support our Troops (as if anti-war people didn't) and nearly every other car had an American flag flying from the door windows. People who spoke out against it were labeled as "Anti-American"; even the Dixie Chicks, who questioned Bush, had their CDs obliterated by a tractor in Louisiana in March 2003 .

The U.S. Congress actually moved to rename the French fries in the House cafeteria to "Freedom fries" to spite anti-war France. The President himself went on TV in prime-time to say that "you're either with us, or with the terrorists."

Lane was one of the few politicians with the guts to speak out against the war. He felt empowered by his own constituents. Of the 250 calls his office received, only seven favored the war. Liberal leaders, however, ignored their constituents and supported the invasion, including Senators Tom Harkin (D-IA), Dianne Feinstein

(D–CA) and Tom Daschle (D–SD).

Lane said the decision to invade Iraq was being rushed, and that the decision should be put off until after Election Day 2002, so citizens could make their voices heard via the ballot box. He made it an issue in his contest against Calderone, who was in full support of the rush to war.

"(The U.S.) should attack as quickly as possible and shouldn't wait for diplomatic efforts with Iraq to fail," Calderone told the *Dispatch/Argus*. "Iraq is a time bomb waiting to happen. The longer we hesitate, the more Saddam Hussein is going to be able to develop more weapons and the better he is going to be able to dig in."

Lane believed Al-Qaeda should be the main target, and this would divert the necessary resources from that fight. For Iraq, he favored diplomacy and sanctions via the United Nations, describing it as a more "constructive approach." As he told the *Dispatch/Argus*: "The better strategy would be to continue the current policy, send in U.N. inspectors, and reconsider the situation if the U.N. concludes Iraq is in violation of its standing resolutions and is nearing a 'real nuclear weapons capability.'" He predicted that Iraq would become a "quagmire of rival ethnic and political rivalries."

In response, Calderone told the media that Lane was "no friend of the military." Anyone who knew Lane, Democrat or Republican, saw right through the claim, and the voters responded accordingly.

With an impressive margin for even a gerrymandered district, Lane crushed Calderone by over fifty thousand votes, 127,093 to 76,519, or 62% to 38%. Calderone congratulated Lane and the two went away on good terms. The *Quad-City Times* said it best in an editorial, stating that Calderone's campaign was a welcome relief from the "diatribes that marked Republican Mark Baker's biennial attempts."

Despite the election win, Lane finally realized that his future on Capitol Hill was limited. So he did something he'd resisted for his entire career. He finally enrolled in the congressional pension plan. He'd get a pension based on his years of enrollment, rather than his years of service. And while he still voted against congressional pay raises and cost-of-living adjustments, he stopped returning the ten percent of his salary to the government. It was time to build up his meager estate.

Lane had few assets and almost no income from other sources. To put that in perspective, Lane's colleague across the river, Jim Leach, had nearly fifteen million dollars in investments, farmland, and business assets. Lane's sole assets were his D.C. townhome, his parents' old house, and a retirement account, all of which totaled about five hundred thousand dollars.

In these later years Lane also began spending more. On his home. His friends. His family. Just not on himself. "Lane is not materialistic and lived like a displaced priest in a way," said Dennis King. "Having money never meant a lot to Lane."

With the money he did have, "he was a little too generous," said Dennis. Lane chipped in for his niece's wedding and college tuition, and he even bought cars for friends and family. He helped out anyone close to him because he could, not because he was forced to. Being generous simply made him feel good.

The years between 2002 and 2004 were relatively quiet for Lane in terms of legislation. He cosponsored a handful of bills that were successful, including the Veterans Health Programs Improvement Act of 2004 and the North Korean Human Rights Act. He was unsuccessful however in initiatives to increase assistance for homeless veterans, fund research on complex multi-trauma injuries in combat, increase G.I. benefits for worker training, and to expand VA home loans.

Much of Lane's time was spent voting against nefarious, profit-seeking bills. He consistently voted to protect the Arctic National Wildlife Refuge from oil and gas exploration, and against deregulation of the banking industry (which led to the 2008 real estate crash).

Lane joined a fight to force U.S. corporations with headquarters overseas to pay their fair share in taxes. He sponsored a bill to deny federal contracts to any company that dodged its taxes.

"While our country was rallying and joining together in the aftermath of September 11, these companies are turning and running," Lane told the *Dispatch/Argus*. "That's outrageous and unfair to the citizens and businesses who pay their fair share in taxes."

Lane also tried to get oil company executives to be prosecuted for price gouging: "Crime in the suites must be equal to crime in the streets." But with an oilman in the White House, that would go nowhere.

One point where he and the Bush administration were in agreement was the Sarbanes–Oxley Act of 2002, which was the result of public outcry following the Enron scandal (in which the energy and commodities company declared bankruptcy based on corporate accounting fraud, leaving thousands holding the bill). The Act tightened regulations on corporate finance reporting and increased independent oversight. It even established a board to oversee the accounting industry and added criminal penalties for corporate accounting fraud.

It was one of Lane's few victories at this time, when a more inquisitive media was starting to ask questions about his health. Reporters were starting to see a decline in Lane, and they made it known in their articles.

In June of 2003 the *Dispatch/Argus* had an article titled "Evans Quietly Goes About His Job," which stated:

"At a recent Capitol Hill event on veterans spending, representatives of various groups took the podium, each dressed in crisp business attire, making strong calls for more money. One man sat on a chair behind them, looking on but seemingly lost in thought. Tie askew, clothes a little rumpled, he stiffly rose to make his comments. Then it became clear this was Rep. Lane Evans, D-Rock Island...He must make concessions to the disease. It primarily affects muscle function, and slows small movements, such as putting the first foot forward to walk. It also inhibits his ability to stand up from a seated position and lowers the volume of his voice."

The public and the press also saw that Lane now needed a full-time handler during the day. Mike Halpin was hired as his driver and scheduler, though his job was really more than that. He was also a secretary, butler, and part-time translator. He accompanied him to meetings and fundraisers, prepped him for constituent events, accompanied him on flights, and tried his best to shield the effects of Parkinson's from the public.

"We not only had to deal with all the political, the legislative and the formal speaking events, but we had to do it across the 17th district from Rock Island to Decatur," recalled Halpin. "He was having more and more bad days and it was due to a lot of the travel. More of a physical thing at that time. Back then he didn't seem to have that kind of cognitive trouble."

Lane's mind was foggy on the little things. The menial tasks and everyday nonsense. But when it came to the things he loved like politics and music he was still sharp.

"We quickly got the XM Radio set up. We'd turn on the sixties channel and cover up the display and see who could name the song first," Halpin said. "He totally kicked my ass."

Lane's health would become a central issue of his next campaign. He would face another retired news personality, Andrea Zinga. She attacked Lane's health right out of the gates at a news conference announcing her candidacy in January of 2004.

"If you feel for Lane Evans, you will not re-elect him," she told reporters. "I think the voters have to ask themselves, are they voting for the person who is best able to be an engaged, 24-7 representative. There are jobs Mr. Evans can do, but being a full-time congressman is one he can't do."

Zinga focused on the issue of Parkinson's even when the subject was a political issue or one of national importance. Like when the results of the 9/11 Commission were presented to Congress, Zinga held a news conference, not to address the results of the Commission: but rather to state that Lane was ninety minutes late to the meeting because of his health. Lane countered by providing evidence that he sat through four-and-a-half hours of testimony and that other congressmembers were late as well.

One of the few times Zinga vocalized her own proposals was to say that she wanted Congress to have oversight over Supreme Court decisions to eliminate all the "activist judges." It was a high-profile issue at the time, as conservative media were attacking lower court decisions on gay marriage and other social issues. It would have been a clear violation of checks and balances, so Lane sarcastically told the media he wondered if Zinga got her law degree at the same place she got her medical degree, since she knew so much about Parkinson's disease as well.

Zinga was coming across poorly in public. Citizens were coming to Lane's defense and saw Zinga as cold-hearted. So as a last-ditch effort, Zinga tried to show her inclusive, caring side during the Rock Island Labor Day parade—one of the first that Lane ever missed. Zinga's parade group was led by a man in a wheelchair carrying a U.S. flag, flanked by two Asian women, two Hispanics, and a black couple. It was so blatant and transparent that some Rock Islanders still laugh about it to this day.

However, Zinga did have one last secret weapon. It was big. The Rock Island County Republicans had filed a complaint with the Federal Elections Committee (FEC) regarding funds raised in the 1998 and 2000 elections. They alleged that Lane had violated campaign finance rules, and the FEC began an investigation.

The complaint alleged that a political action committee called the 17th District Victory Fund was an "alter ego" of Lane's official campaign committee, the Friends of Lane Evans. The Victory Fund was established to gather donations for Democratic candidates throughout the district, including state representative, county board seats, and others, including Lane's congressional campaign. Republicans accused the Victory Fund of violating campaign spending limits and stockpiling donations from one campaign year to the next.

As staffer Jeremiah Posedel recalled: "The Victory Fund honestly helped all the candidates. If you register someone and get them out to vote, the hope is that they don't just vote for Lane and stop, they continue their way down the ballot. Lane was clearly the main candidate, but I would say most of our actions benefited the entire ticket."

The entire complaint was based on a technicality, according to Dennis King: "The facts were not in dispute. The FEC was alleging that there was so much control over the Victory Fund by the Friends of Lane Evans committee that it was an arm of the Evans campaign. Technically, there wasn't a separate board to allocate the funds. It was under control of the same people working for the Friends of Lane Evans. But if you look at the format that was done, everything was done according to the rules."

Lane had a team of lawyers examine the Victory Fund before it was even formed. The Victory Fund was technically legal at the time. Years later, though, the McCain-Feingold bill would ban such activities.

"None of us expected that the FEC would say a local county party can't actively campaign for all the candidates on its ticket, including the federal ones," said Eric Nelson. "There had never been any restrictions on county parties campaigning for everyone on the party ticket."

Voters were not swayed by the FEC scandal. On November 2, 2004, Lane trounced Zinga 172,320 to 111,680, or 61% to 39%. Lane knew that the voters had been clearly upset by Zinga's attacks on his health. In his victory speech, he made a point of calling out Zinga for attacking his disability: "It's a disgrace. The disabled population in the Quad Cities and throughout the district reached out to me. I hope we've all learned that people shouldn't be held back for a disability."

A few months after the election, Lane put an end to the FEC investigation. The Friends of Lane Evans agreed to pay the FEC a fine of $185,000 without admitting guilt. The judge went on record to say that he believed Lane's group had violated the law, but it would never be played out in court.

"Lane took it very seriously," Dennis said. "He was going to hire the Bower attorneys, which were legal counsel to the president. They are the best in election law and their price is commensurate. It would have cost hundreds of thousands of dollars to represent the case. Lane believed that people contributed to his campaign so he can campaign, not to fight some legal battle."

Lane's true defense would have never held up in court. He believed the Victory Fund was necessary to counteract all the massive personal donations coming in from corporations and wealthy Republicans. It was meant to give middle-class donors equal footing against the rich, based on a technicality, and it failed.

This pretty much set the precedent for Lane's final years in office. His body was failing. His mind was wandering. His private and personal information that he held so dear would soon be splashed across the media.

Chapter Nineteen

The White Album

December 7, 2011: Lane was moved to the Hope Creek Care Center in East Moline, which was owned and operated by Rock Island County. The facility had its northern wing named after Lane, but he was residing in the southern wing, right off the community area and within shouting distance of the nurses' station. He was basically in a glorified hospital room with a few shelves and dresser-drawer for his belongings.

I drove in town from Omaha to see how he was doing. After the visit, I sent an email to Erin and some of his other old friends:

"You may or may not know that Lane has been moved to Hope Creek Care Center. While some people feared this would be a detrimental move, I would like to tell you he is being VERY well cared for. At his past residence, he was sitting in front of the TV for most of the day. Now at Hope Creek, he is getting physical therapy every day and spends his afternoons in a community room where he can watch people or interact. Also, he is dressed up more often, wearing nice collared shirts, dress pants, and his congressional loafers. I have noticed a definite decline in his speech and mobility in the past year, yet this move has given him a new spark. I visited him today for the first time in a long time and I was very impressed with his care. As I said, though his physical health is declining, he seems more intellectually stimulated. Plus, he has some very cute nurses encouraging him."

It was all true, though slightly embellished. He was still usually dressed in sweatpants and he had most of his meals fed to him in his room, but he did have daily trips to his physical therapy sessions and was often wheeled into the community room for socializing. Lane was clearly doing much better and I was thankful he once again had 24-hour care. Overall, it seemed like he had his dignity back.

Summer 2014: Two years passed and I saw Lane twice during this time. Once he was passed out in a wheelchair in the community room as all the other residents played Hangman. The other time, he was asleep in the fitness room awaiting his workout.

One weekend that summer Cher called me in Omaha and said: "It's only a matter of time, Devin. Can you write his obituary?"

I told her, "Of course." Then I drove four hours to see him one last time.

As usual, there was no security. I walked right to his room. His eyes were closed, and he was tucked beneath the USMC blanket I gave him years ago.

For a moment, I thought I might be too late. I put my finger on his neck to find a pulse. He gasped, and his eyes sprung open in terror. I took a step back and laughed with relief.

"Hey Lane, long time no see," I smiled.

His face didn't move. I wondered if he recognized me, or if time was still suspended.

"I just came to say hello."

He stared at me as though I were a monster that had followed him out of a nightmare.

"It's me, Lane. It's Devin."

His face softened and he finally blinked. He didn't look as sickly as I thought he would. In fact, I didn't see much of a difference at all. But I had been gone for so long, I didn't know the details of his condition.

"Wanna hear some music?" I went over to the wall unit and flipped through his collection of music CDs. There were only four. All of them were by The Beatles, of course.

I put the White Album into a small boombox and pulled up a chair beside him.

A nurse appeared in the doorway.

"We're old friends," I told her, pointing at the photo of Lane, Obama, Cher and I on the dresser. She smiled and slowly pulled the door closed.

As the music started, I could literally see the stress leave his face. He smiled, bathing in the comfortable harmony.

We listened to the entire album. Sometimes he sang along in a faint off-key mumble. Other times he'd close his eyes and hum. The music was like a maternal comfort, swaddling him in peace and tranquility.

When it was over, I played the album again. I'd play it all day if it made him feel this way. This time, though, he was going in and out of consciousness. At one point I leaned over and confessed, "I hate the Beatles, Lane."

I half-expected him to snap to attention and start choking me. But he stayed asleep. Probably dreaming of tangerine trees and marmalade skies. Running through strawberry fields. Warm guns and weeping guitars. His own private Heaven.

The album ended. He was in a deep asleep. One final lullaby.

I went over and touched his hand.

"Goodbye, Lane."

November 5, 2014: Weeks went by. I waited every day for the news, yet nothing. The leaves turned color. My wife was transferred again, and we moved back to the Quad Cities. And Lane was somehow still alive.

I didn't go see him, though. I was afraid of what I might see or find. The goodbye we'd shared already felt so perfect that I wanted to remember him that way.

Finally, on the morning of November 5th, I got a call from Cher. I knew what she was going to say before I answered.

"I'm sorry," I told her. I felt no sadness. No pity nor loss. His pain was over.

His funeral was on November 10, 2014 at Sacred Heart Catholic Church in Moline. A massive stone church that was only half-filled. His old friend Rep. Jan Schakowsky gave a eulogy, as did Phil Hare, Rep. David Bonior (D-MI), and current 17th District Representative, Democrat Cheri Bustos. Phil was overwhelmed with emotion and stumbled through his speech. Bustos spoke as if she were on the campaign trail, talking more about herself than Lane. And Bonior topped them all by ending his speech with a quote from the Beatles: "In the end, the love you take is equal to the love you make."

I left the funeral mass early so I could get to the Rock Island Arsenal Cemetery. I parked at the other end of the cemetery where my father was buried; a few hundred yards from the northern gazebo where mourners gather for the final ceremonies. After a few minutes, the motorcade arrived, his family and friends sat in folding chairs and a U.S. flag was draped over Lane's casket. I stayed out of sight. This was a time for his closest loved ones.

A middle-aged woman in yoga pants came over and stood beside me.

"Is that Lane Evans?" she said, taking a sip from her water bottle.

"Yes."

"Are you family?" she asked, looking at my dark blue trenchcoat that used to be Lane's.

"No, I just went to the funeral."

"He was a great man."

"True."

161

"There's a lot of great men in this cemetery."

I smiled. She and I stood there and silently watched the rest of the ceremony. A bugler played Taps. The Color Guard raised their rifles and fired off a triple-volley salute. Two Marines folded the casket flag into a taut triangle. A spent shell was tucked into the flag and an officer formally presented it to the family.

After several hugs and salutes, everyone walked solemnly back to their cars.

Lane was laid to rest among his brethren.

Chapter Twenty

The End

The 109th Congress of the United States was uneventful for both Lane and the Democrats. They were called the "Do Nothing" Congress, a term not used since the days of Harry Truman, when a similar Congress accomplished absolutely nothing.

President Bush was serving the first two years of his second term in the White House and neither party could agree on anything of substance. Not to mention, the stream of flag-draped caskets returning from Iraq was wearing on the American public. The response to Hurricane Katrina was a disgrace. Lending deregulation and a boom in subprime mortgages would result in a catastrophic burst of the housing bubble. And the prominence of sex and fundraising scandals led Rolling Stone to dub Congress "a stable of thieves and perverts."

The two parties focused more on blame and accusations than working together to find collective, mutually acceptable solutions to the country's ills. They were like two parents in the early stages of divorce. Foreshadowing their own atrocities by accusing the other party of those same misdeeds: "Yeah, I cheated, but only because you did it first." Distract, deflect, and demean the opposition so you can hide your own crimes.

One of the few things they agreed upon was the deplorable Military Commissions Act of 2006, which essentially granted the federal government permission to indefinitely imprison anyone deemed a terrorist, even a U.S. citizen, without due process. Lane and 160 other Democrats voted against it, along with Jim Leach and notable libertarians like Rep. Ron Paul (R-TX).

Looking back, it was a resurgence of the 1968 divide. A renewed fissure between the two parties based on greed, sloth, and pride, all while increasing the power of the U.S. government and its corporate sponsors.

Maybe it was a good time for Lane to bow out. Even if a man like him was needed more than ever...

In January of 2006, Lane's part-time girlfriend OkCha prodded him on the issue of Korean comfort women. She asked that he go to Korea and speak with dignitaries there. He obliged and from January 20th to 28th he traveled to South Korea with OkCha, Dennis King, and a small number of staffers.

The first few days, they visited the embassies and met with the South Korean secretary of state and other ambassadors.

"We learned about Korea and U.S. trade policy," Dennis recalled. "Lane gave his strong views on fair trade and told them that our workers were getting screwed by foreign competition."

Lane then visited U.S. troops in the Demilitarized Zone (DMZ) to review their living conditions and show moral support. After that, he traveled to a few fundraisers and meetings arranged by OkCha. Lane was celebrated for his work on the comfort women issue, and even received an honorary doctorate from Kosin University for his endeavors.

"He accomplished things on that trip," said King. "Ameri-Asian issues, visa issues, comfort women, he helped them a lot. It was a wonderful trip, but very exhausting. His body rebelled a bit."

On the long plane ride back to the U.S., Lane's strength finally gave out.

"He was doing really badly. It was too much for him to take the trip. I observe him react very badly. He was falling on (airport) elevator," recalled OkCha.

Lane was immediately hospitalized at the Bethesda Naval Hospital, also known as the Walter Reed National Military Medical Center. He was unconscious and running a high fever. The doctors were perplexed. "I was with the doctors a lot," said Dennis. "They didn't know what was going on either. We had met with the neurologist a week before going to Korea, and he didn't tell him not to go. Travel is difficult. It really throws Parkinson's out of kilter."

After a few days, Lane regained consciousness. But he was still unresponsive. Dennis called Phil Hare and asked him to fly out and try to break Lane out of his trance.

"I went to see him. He was laying and wouldn't open his eyes," Phil recalled. "I sat by the bed; he looked horrible. I said to him, 'I didn't fly seven hundred miles for you to be rude. What the hell's the deal here? Just open up one eye so I know you are still breathing.'"

Lane awoke and started to cry. He told Phil he was letting everyone down. "Who, us?" Phil had said. "No, the constituents," Lane replied.

"Then I told him, 'I'm coming back here every day until you start eating, and I will stay here,'" Phil recalled. And over the course of a week, Lane did recover. The doctors stripped him of all medications and started over. Lane began eating again and talking, albeit quiet and disjointed. "I stayed with him until he was discharged. I thought we were going to have to start looking at nursing homes," said Phil.

For the next few weeks, OkCha cared for Lane at his townhouse and Erin returned from California to help. "When he crashed, Erin came to see if she could help," Malmstrom recalled, "Between the two of them they took care of him. They helped him through."

By early February, Lane had regained most of his strength. Lane's spokesman Steve Vetzner said the mystery illness was "fatigue," and Lane made his first appearance back at the office. His staff recalled seeing a distinct change in Lane, however. His voice was quieter. He got confused more easily. For the first time they saw him drool on himself. Everyone did their best to shield his condition from the media.

On February 14th, Lane cast one vote. The next day, he was hospitalized with exhaustion. Doctors released him within twenty-four hours and ordered him to stay in bed. Lane then went back to his home in Rock Island and his brother Doyle cared for him.

Weeks passed, and Lane had all but disappeared from the public eye. He had a historically high voting record, usually over 97 percent, yet he had cast just 9 out of 81 votes for the first three months of 2006; an absence rate of nearly 90 percent. The local newspapers began running several articles and editorials questioning the congressman's absence, especially since a primary election was coming up on March 21.

"His doctors felt that taking time away from the office would help in better managing his Parkinson's," spokesman Steve Vetzner told the *Dispatch/Argus*. "He wants to get some rest but also wants to make sure he's in top shape for the weeks and months ahead." He said that Lane would be returning to Congress on March 27th, after the Congressional recess.

On March 21, the Illinois primaries were held. Lane ran uncontested and won with 38,780 votes.

Then six days later, when Congress reconvened, Lane made a surprise announcement via a press release:

This is a tough day for me. I am announcing that I will not run for re-election and will retire at the end of my current term in the U.S. House of Representatives.

When I announced in 1998 that I had Parkinson's Disease, my doctor said that this condition would not interfere with my work and that I would be able to perform at a high level for a number of years. That window of opportunity is now closing.

I fully expected that I would continue my work for the foreseeable future following this current break from the office. But I have come to recognize that the time needed to address my health makes it difficult to wage a campaign and carry out my work as representative. I will return soon and to the best of my ability, complete the important work of this term in my role as representative and Ranking Member of the House Committee on Veterans' Affairs.

This decision is especially tough because this job means so much to me. I believe strongly in serving people and working to make a positive difference in their lives. Every day has been rewarding and I'm proud of what I've been able to accomplish and the fights I've made.

I thank my family and everyone who has worked with me—great friends, terrific colleagues, a dedicated staff, fellow vets. And I appreciate the support of people I never met before who would ask how I was doing and tell me to keep up the good fight. I'll be doing that in the weeks and months ahead and look forward to thanking every one of you personally for all you have meant to me.

To my constituents and veterans across this country, it is an honor and privilege to represent you.

Semper Fi,

Lane

The decision was met with sadness and respect. Politicians from all spectrums released statements in his support:

"Lane has valiantly battled Parkinson's disease for the past decade. I wish him Godspeed as he continues this battle and I ask everyone to please keep Lane Evans in your thoughts and prayers."
— *U.S. Rep. Ray LaHood, R-Ill.*

"He has approached his disease with dignity, class and courage, and he has served as an inspiration to others with Parkinson's disease."
— *U.S. Rep. Luis Gutierrez, D-Ill.*

"No one has been a better advocate for veterans than Lane Evans. Americans in uniform will miss him in the Congress."
— *U.S. Rep. Mark Kirk, R-Ill.*

"Lane finally realized that he couldn't campaign again," said former staffer Jerry Lack: "He felt he could serve out the term, but not campaign. He agonized over it for several weeks. It shocked the whole staff when he finally made that decision."

The Democrats would have to elect a replacement. And the Illinois State Board of Elections stated that, by law, the election would be held among the precinct committeemen, rather than another primary election.

Lane immediately endorsed Phil Hare as his successor. Six other candidates stepped forward, including Rock Island Mayor Mark Schwiebert. Schwiebert seemed to be the choice among the everyday voter. He was the name most mentioned in the coffee shops and taverns, and he even won an official poll conducted by the 17th District State Central Committee office with 11 percent of the vote. Phil Hare came in last in that poll with just 6 percent.

Both the *Quad-City Times* and the *Dispatch/Argus* also endorsed Mark Schwiebert as the nominee, and published their criticism of the upcoming election process. The *Quad-City Times* wrote on April 14, 2006:

"Evans' successor will be selected by nameless, rank-and-file party workers who dutifully show up at party functions, hustle countless fundraising raffle tickets and do the unpaid work to help keep Democrats in office. Most of those precinct committeemen got their jobs at the invitation of John Gianulis. Gianulis removed any semblance of an open process by hand-picking Evans' successor, and hand-picking most of the precinct committeemen who will make the decision. Credit Gianulis for consistency. That's the way things have always been done since assuming county chairmanship in 1968. This 2006 problem deserves better than a 1968 solution."

The mail-in election was held in June 2006. Phil Hare won and Schwiebert came in third.

Many in the public believed it was a conspiracy that had been months in the making. Everything seemed too coincidental. Defenders pointed out that Lane he had been raising money for months and had assigned his staff campaign duties. "We weren't smart enough to plan it as it happened," Dennis King said. "Lane did not want to leave office. No desire. He wanted to continue serving."

However, it had played out in nearly the same way that Rep. Daniel Lipinski inherited the IL-3 U.S. Congressional seat from his father Bill Lipinski two years earlier in August of 2004 -- Bill announced his retirement after winning the Democratic primary and Dan was nominated by a small group of Democratic party leaders including the notorious Illinois House Speaker Michael Madigan, Cook County Board member John Daley and Bill Lipinski himself.

In an interview with the *Dispatch/Argus*, Lane discussed the timing of his retirement: "I think I knew it before the actual primary, but I didn't really internalize it. I think it is a very humbling illness to go through. It's hard to understand what you're going through. When it became evident that I wouldn't be able to do the job I wanted to, that is when I decided it was best to go forward (and announce my retirement)."

The early Illinois primaries also contributed to the circumstances. Candidates have to file election papers in December (the year prior to the election), primaries are in March, and the general election is months later in November. It creates an endless cycle of campaigning for Congressional terms that last just two years.

In this author's opinion, Lane didn't have a master plan to retire and coronate Phil. He didn't have the mental wherewithal at the time. That being said, it doesn't mean those around him didn't play the system.

"It felt like we were trying to hide (Lane's) sickness during the primary, and I disagreed with that. I would have rather seen him go out on top," said Jerry Lack. "For his legacy, it would have been better if it worked out that way."

On November 6, 2006, Phil Hare defeated Andrea Zinga in the general election, 57 percent to 43 percent, or 114,638 to 85,734. Dennis King remained as Chief of Staff, and so did much of the staff that worked in constituent services.

Meanwhile, Lane still had several months left to serve. He had been recovering at his Rock Island home since mid-February and returned to D.C. in June to cast a handful of votes. Then he suddenly fell ill again, and returned to Rock Island.

Constituents and the media wondered if he had the ability to finish his term. Not only was he missing Congressional votes and committee meetings, he had also handed over his personal and financial affairs to his brothers.

Back in April 2006, shortly after he announced his retirement, Lane had petitioned the Rock Island County circuit court to appoint Doyle and Steve as his temporary limited guardians so they could sign legal documents on his behalf. The petition stated: "The Respondent was recently in the hospital for complications due to Parkinson's disease and has limited mobility and intermittent cognitive impairments." Judge Alan Blackwood granted the petition and it went immediately into effect.

It was the first time Lane's mental state had been addressed publicly. The *Dispatch/Argus* asked if "the description meant that the congressman is unable to think clearly." Lane's spokesman Vetzner again replied that it was "just fatigue."

A permanent guardianship hearing was set for June 9, 2006, the same month that Phil won the special election. Lane's brothers now sought to become his permanent guardians and control all of his affairs. Lane objected, though didn't vocalize his reasons. He hired his own representation, Attorney Art Winstein (son of Lane's mentor

Stewart Winstein), sparking a range of public rumors and speculations. Some talked of a long-time family dispute, others claimed a secret marriage to OkCha, and many said it was a fierce battle over a phantom estate worth "millions" (Lane's actual holdings only totaled about $700,000).

Lane and his brothers refused to talk to the media, which only added fuel to the rumors. "I'm not gonna talk about my family," Lane told the press.

At the hearing, Judge Blackwood issued a surprise ruling that neither his brothers nor Lane would control his estate. Lane was issued new guardians: American Bank would manage his financial affairs and Dennis King would be in charge of his personal matters. Following the decision, Lane and his brothers issued a joint statement: "The family is glad this matter has resolved itself amicably. The family believes this resolution is in the best interest of all parties involved." Winstein added: "No hard feelings, no family split, there were no issues at any point in time."

Only Lane, his brothers and the lawyers would ever know what truly happened, because the day of the hearing, attorney John Mc-Gehee (a friend of Lane's who had been appointed his guardian ad litem) filed a motion to close the courtroom to the public and the media. Judge Blackwood agreed, and additionally ordered the court records to be sealed.. The *Associated Press*, the *Dispatch/Argus* and the *Quad City Times* all filed a petition appealing the decision on the grounds that the public had a right to know the medical condition of their sitting congressman.

At that hearing on July 26, 2006, Judge Blackwood issued a split decision. He reaffirmed that the medical records remain sealed and gag orders stay in effect, but did allow the transcripts of the hearing to be released. The press reviewed those transcripts, and unfortunately there was no new information nor revelations.

A month passed, and Lane stayed in Rock Island to recuperate. He soon cut ties with OkCha so he could focus on his health and physical therapy. He was also taking new medications and his awareness had dramatically improved. In mid-September he surprised everyone by returning to D.C. and casting a handful of votes. He had missed 476 of 516 votes since January. The votes he cast were of little consequence, however, and he voted along the party line.

It was Lane's last stint in D.C. After a few days, he was exhausted again. He took one last tour of the city and said goodbye to his colleagues and friends. He sold his townhouse (and a small condo in Florida), and moved all his belongings back to the Quad Cities in a single van. There were no parties nor parades. He quietly returned home to live out his final years. Phil Hare was sworn in on January

3, 2007.

Soon enough though, Lane found himself in the news again. In March 2007, Dennis King relinquished guardianship to Cher Erickson and Mike Malmstrom. John McGehee had asked them both to be Lane's permanent guardians, as Dennis was just a fill-in. They would handle Lane's day-to-day affairs and American Bank was still in charge of his finances. Lane's pension would go mostly to his care and boarding. After expenses, he had a few hundred dollars each month in spending money.

Meanwhile, Lane was getting accolades throughout the community. He had a post office in Rock Island named after him and a small trophy case was erected in the Rock Island County building. Genesis Health Center dedicated a gazebo in his honor and Lane's name was added to the veterans education center at Black Hawk College. Even the street he grew up on was renamed Lane Evans Drive.

Occasionally he would attend a local campaign event or party, but mostly he stayed home. In August of 2008 he attended an invite-only rally in Davenport for Obama's presidential campaign. There, Obama told the crowd: "If it weren't for this man, I can certainly say I wouldn't be standing before you today. I don't think I would've won the United States Senate race. He's a great congressman and a great friend."

Soon Lane moved into the Lighthouse in Silvis. He had a nice, large apartment. A view of the cornfields. A caretaker by his side. One cold day in December, he would tell me his story.

CPSIA information can be obtained
at www.ICGtesting.com
Printed in the USA
BVHW071448071019
560429BV00009B/711/P